THE VOICE OF POVERTY

THE VOICE OF POVERTY

THE HIDDEN WAR FOR POWER

How Truth Was Reversed, Who Runs the World, and the Path to Reclamation

SAMUEL MESSIAS

Library of Congress Control Number: 2026903513
Paperback ISBN: 979-8-9952418-0-5
Hardcover ISBN: 979-8-9952418-2-9
eBook ISBN: 979-8-9952418-1-2

Cover design: Samuel Messias
The pictures shown were generated using artificial intelligence.
www.voiceofpoverty.com

Printed in the United States of America

10 9 8 7 6 5 4 3 2 1

Isaiah 28:9 (KJV)—"Whom shall he teach knowledge? And whom shall he make to understand doctrine? them that are weaned from the milk, and drawn from the breasts."

Matthew 13:11 (KJV)—"He answered and said unto them, Because it is given unto you to know the mysteries of the kingdom of heaven, but to them it is not given."

Contents

Part Three: The Path To Reclamation

Author's Note

THIS BOOK IS NOT WRITTEN TO PROVOKE CONFLICT, BUT TO awaken clarity. *The Voice of Poverty—The Hidden War for Power* was born from a place of spiritual hunger—a deep, burning need to understand why poverty persists, why power is hoarded, and why truth feels so often buried beneath layers of tradition, religion, and fear.

What you're about to read challenges mainstream theology. It re-examines biblical stories with fresh eyes. It speaks to Black divinity, not to exclude others, but to reclaim what has long been distorted, denied, or stolen. This is not about hate. It's about healing. It's not about race or skin color but spiritual identity and the divine right to know who we are.

I understand this book may be controversial to some. It questions religious narratives that have gone unquestioned for centuries. It reinterprets the serpent in Eden, reframes Jesus in nontraditional ways, and dares to say that the poor are not powerless—they are spiritually targeted. To those who disagree, I welcome your questions—not for debate, but for dialogue. My goal is not to convert anyone. My mission is to shine a light where silence has lived too long.

May this work be a mirror to the soul, a torch for those walking in darkness, and a key for those who feel locked out of divine truth.

In truth, in courage,
Samuel Messias
Founder, Voice of Poverty LLC
www.voiceofpoverty.com

Introduction:
The Awakening

THERE'S A QUESTION THAT LINGERS IN THE MINDS OF MANY, though few dare to ask it aloud: *Why are Black people so hated?*

Why have the original people—the first creation—been the most oppressed, the most erased, the most vilified throughout history?

The answer is not what you've been told. It is not slavery, it is not colonization, it is not economic inequality. Those are just symptoms. The disease is something far more profound. Something spiritual. Something ancient.

For centuries, a grand deception has been at work, flipping the truth upside down and replacing it with a lie so massive that even those who suffer under it defend it. Yet the time of ignorance is over. The time of waking up is now.

This book is not here to make you comfortable. It is not here to play by the rules of those who stole knowledge, rewrote history, and designed a system to keep Black people asleep. This book is here to tell the truth, and the truth is this: Black people were the original creation, formed by the true Creator.

But an opposing force—whether you call it Satan, a demiurge, or something else—created its version of man, a counterfeit, designed to rule this world through deception and control.

The evidence has been hidden in plain sight. It is in the Bible, twisted by those who wanted to use it as a tool for submission rather than enlightenment. It is in history, buried under false narratives and whitewashed textbooks. And it is in the world today where the ruling powers of this system operate exactly as you would expect if they were created to dominate, deceive, and suppress the first people.

Yet now, the veil is lifting. Now, the spell is breaking. This book will take you deep into the real story of creation—who was made first and who came after. It will expose the true identity of the serpent in the Garden of Eden and why it was demonized. It will reveal the hidden rulers of this world and how they maintain power.

Most importantly, it will show the path to *reclaiming what was stolen*. This is not just a book. This is a *war cry*. Because the battle for knowledge is the battle for power, and once you see the truth, you can never unsee it.

The awakening begins now.

PART ONE

The Hidden Creation Story

Plate I — First Creation

Chapter 1
The First Creation

The First Creation—The Divine Origin Before the Split

The world has handed you a single version of history—a filtered, diluted narrative designed to keep you blind. But beneath the surface of religious doctrine and historical manipulation lies a truth older than nations, older than race, older than suffering itself. A truth deliberately buried: Black people were not an afterthought of creation. They were the First Creation—beings of pure light, consciousness, and divine frequency. Before Genesis 2 introduced the world to restriction, hierarchy, and control, there existed a creation untouched by fear. To understand the war between the two creations, we must return to the beginning—not the version taught in schools or pulpits, but the original blueprint spoken by the Creator of peace and balance.

What Was the First Creation Like?

Genesis 1 is not a primitive myth or symbolic poem. It is the record of a perfect creation brought into existence by Elohim, the spiritual Creator. Everything in this chapter reveals a world utterly different from what appears in Genesis 2—and different from the world we know today. This first creation was harmonious, unified, and spiritually awake.

Life for the Beings of Genesis 1

The beings created in Genesis 1 were not rough, incomplete, or limited. They were the reflection of Elohim's own essence:

- Male and female were created simultaneously.
- Balanced in purpose and authority.
- Endowed with inner light and higher consciousness.

They were connected directly to the Source without an intermediary. They were beings whose very existence radiated with divine intelligence. They did not "learn" from experience—they remembered from within.

They lived in a world without:

- Fear
- Shame
- Punishment
- Hierarchy
- Violence
- Bloodshed

Before the lesser god appeared, there were no curses, no commandments, no forbidden trees—only freedom and creative power.

Their Abilities: Living as Divine Reflections with Spiritual Intuition

Because they were made "in the image of God," they carried Elohim's consciousness. "In the image" never meant physical resemblance. It meant:

- Same frequency
- Same awareness
- Same creative ability
- Same internal light

They could sense intention, perceive energy, and understand the natural laws instinctively. They operated through intuition, not instruction.

Co-Creation with Elohim

Genesis 1:28 says they were blessed—not commanded—to multiply, to replenish, and to have dominion. This was not domination through force, but co-creation through harmony. Their dominion was not ownership. It was stewardship. They worked in unity with the Creator, participating in the unfolding of creation itself. Their thoughts and words carried power. Their energy shaped their environment.

Vibrational Harmony

Before the fall into physical limitation, these beings understood vibration. They lived in alignment with:

- The frequency of love
- The rhythm of nature
- The balance of masculine and feminine energies
- The spiritual laws governing creation

There was no competition between man and woman, tribe and tribe, or nature and humanity. All moved as one body with one purpose.

Communication: Spirit-to-Spirit

The First Creation didn't communicate through sound or language. Their communication was:

- Telepathic
- Heart-centered
- Spirit-to-spirit
- Frequency-based

They could feel the truth without debate. They could sense intention without speech. They could understand creation without instruction. No lies existed because deception itself had not been born.

Their Relationship with Elohim

The relationship between Elohim and the First Creation was intimate, direct, and non-hierarchical.

- Elohim did not command them—Elohim blessed them.

- Elohim did not restrict them—Elohim empowered them.
- Elohim did not hide from them—Elohim dwelt within them.

There was no mediator, no prophet, no priest, no temple. *They themselves were temples.* The kingdom of God was already within them, long before Christ later confirmed, "The kingdom of God is within you."

Their Connection to Nature and Energy

The First Creation lived in a world where nature wasn't a resource—it was a conscious partner. Every herb-bearing seed and every fruit-bearing tree was given for their nourishment. This simple detail reveals a world without:

- Killing
- Sacrifice
- Predators
- Bloodshed

Energy flowed without blockage. Creation cooperated willingly.

The earth itself fed their bodies and spirits.

Nature was an extension of their own consciousness.

Their Original Purpose

The purpose of the First Creation was not obedience, worship, or servitude. Their purpose was:

- To manifest Elohim on Earth
- To maintain balance in creation

- To multiply light, not flesh alone.
- To keep the earth in harmony
- To awaken creation through consciousness

They were the bridge between spirit and matter.

Humanity was never meant to descend into fear, shame, or separation. That came later—when another being entered the scene. Why? These points are for Black people as the First Creation. This part of the truth has been hidden most aggressively because it is the key to liberation.

1. Scientific Evidence

Anthropologists agree that the earliest human remains—the oldest on Earth—come from Africa.

- The oldest bones
- The earliest civilizations
- The first language systems
- The first mathematical structures.

All arise from the same source: *Blackness.*

2. Melanin as Divine Technology

Melanin is not a biological accident. It is:

- An energy conductor
- A regulator of light
- An absorber of radiation
- A transmitter of frequency

It is spiritual technology, something the First Creation beings would require in a world of pure light and vibrational coherence.

3. Ancient Spiritual Traditions

Ancient African cosmologies—from Kemet to Nubia to Ethiopia—teach:

- Humans were divine beings.
- Communication was spiritual, not verbal.
- Light and consciousness were central to creation.
- Humanity originally lived in balance, not hierarchy.
- These traditions align perfectly with the Genesis 1 creation.

4. The Global Obsession with Black Suppression

The unnatural, irrational hatred toward Black skin is not based on inferiority—it is based on a forgotten threat. If the First Creation was divine and if Black people descend from that divine line, then the systems built by the second creation must suppress that identity at any cost. The greatest threat to a counterfeit god is people who remember who they are.

Why Should You Believe This?

Ask yourself:

- Why does Genesis 1 describe a perfect creation and Genesis 2 immediately contradict it?
- Why does the name of the Creator suddenly change?
- Why does the second god introduce fear, rules, curses, and death?
- Why does the world system hate the very people whose DNA points to the origins of humanity?

- Why does every institution—from religion to science to government—fight to suppress this knowledge?

Because remembering the First Creation exposes the counterfeit.

Because awakening reveals that oppression was engineered to keep divine people asleep.

Because the greatest weapon against a false ruler is truth.

Leading into Chapter Two: The Other Creation

Now that we understand the purity, power, and purpose of the First Creation, we can finally turn to the mystery that has confused believers for centuries: If creation was complete in Genesis 1, what is Genesis 2?

Who is the LORD God?

Why is there suddenly a different version of humanity—formed instead of spoken, controlled instead of empowered?

Chapter Two uncovers the other creation—the beginning of hierarchy, fear, physical limitation, and spiritual captivity.

The birth of the system that still rules the world today. The awakening continues.

Plate II — Other Creation

Chapter 2
The Other Creation

The Other Creation—The Deception Begins

Let's be clear from the start: the story we've been told about humanity's creation is incomplete. The version preached in churches, taught in schools, and used to justify slavery and colonialism is not the entire truth. It is, at best, a half-truth—and at worst, a deliberate deception. This being—unlike Elohim—did not create through light or consciousness. He formed from the dust. He commanded. He restricted. He punished. This was a creator of limits, not liberation.

A Lower Being, Not the Source

The LORD God was not the First Source. He was a finite being operating within a dimension beneath the highest realm of Elohim. He was a craftsman-god—shaping matter, manipulating form, and constructing a controlled environment. He could not spark divinity; he could only sculpt flesh. Where Elohim created beings who were whole, conscious, intuitive, and eternal, the LORD God produced a creation that required his supervision, his rules, and his breath to survive.

A Jealous Nature

Unlike Elohim, who is complete and lacks nothing, the LORD God desired worship.

He desired obedience.

He desired control.

His jealousy was not divine anger—it was insecurity.

A being who is whole does not fear losing power.

A being who is unstable fears everything.

Where Did This Being Come From?

Ancient spiritual traditions—Kemet, early Ethiopia, the Gnostic texts, and several African cosmologies—speak of a lesser being who tried to imitate the true Creator. This being, having discovered the energetic blueprint of creation, attempted to replicate it—building a physical world that mirrored the spiritual one, populating it with beings who would depend on him, and ultimately seeking to trap souls within form. This explains the sudden shift between Genesis 1 and Genesis 2.

We are no longer observing Elohim's cosmos.

We are observing another realm under a different authority.

Why the Second Creator Made a New Creation

The LORD God required:

- Servants, not sovereigns
- Obedience, not partnership
- Worship, not harmony
- Control, not consciousness

The First Creation could never serve him—they were divine, complete, equal in essence to Elohim. He needed another line of humans that would fear him, depend on him, listen to him, and remain bound to physicality. This is why he formed a being from dust—a symbol of limitation and mortality. Thus, the Second Creation begins.

Genesis 2 as a Counterfeit Creation

Genesis 2 is not a continuation; it is a different story altogether. And every detail exposes the difference.

Dust vs. Light

Genesis 1 beings:

- Created in the image of Elohim
- Made of light, consciousness, and spiritual essence
- Eternal and unrestricted

Genesis 2 beings:

- Made of dust, the lowest form of matter
- Bound to the physical

- Dependent on the LORD God's breath
- Limited awareness

Dust symbolizes:

- Decay
- Obedience
- Mortality
- Separation from spiritual memory

Rib = Hierarchy

- In Genesis 1, male and female are created together.
- They are equal, unified, and balanced.

In the counterfeit creation:

- Woman is formed from a man.
- Woman is defined by absence and dependency.
- Patriarchy is introduced.

This is not divine order. This is an imposed hierarchy.

The Garden = A Controlled Environment

Eden was not paradise. It was a controlled test site:

- Fenced in
- Monitored
- Restricted
- Conditioned

Unlike the vastness of Creation in Genesis 1, Eden is a place where knowledge is forbidden and obedience is demanded.

Commandments = Fear-Based System Instead of Freedom

- Warnings are given.
- Punishments are assigned.
- Threats are introduced.

This is the first sign of the LORD God's nature: control through fear.

Shame Is Introduced

Before the LORD God's creation, shame did not exist. Genesis 2–3 introduces:

- Shame
- Guilt
- Impurity
- Moral punishment

These psychological tools are the markers of control-based religions.

Clothing = Consciousness

Falls into Materiality

Elohim's creation was clothed with light. The LORD God's creation is clothed with skins. This symbolizes:

- Loss of spiritual sight
- Descent into physical identity
- Separation from the Creator
- The beginning of forgetfulness

Genesis 2 is not an improvement. It is confinement.

How the Two Lineages Formed and Diverged

Genesis reveals a world where the First Creation still existed outside the Garden.

The First Creation lived freely, maintained spiritual consciousness, continued in harmony with Elohim, and remained outside the LORD God's imposed system. These people were never placed under Edenic law.

- They were never cursed.
- They were never told they were naked.
- They were never commanded to obey.

The Second Creation: Adam, Eve, and their offspring lived under the LORD God.

- Shame
- Obedience
- Fear
- Physical limitation

Their lineage was shaped by trauma and hierarchy.

The Lineages Collide—Through Cain

This becomes the first bridge between the two creations, yet also the first evidence that these lineages were never meant to merge.

Cain in the Land of Nod—The Forbidden Mystery

The Bible leaves a hole wide enough to expose the hidden truth:

- Cain kills Abel.
- Cain is cursed.

- Cain is cast out.
- Cain goes to Nod.
- Cain finds a wife.
- Cain builds a city.

How?

Who Was Cain Spiritually?

Cain was the perfect expression of the Second Creator's nature:

- Restless
- Angry
- Competitive
- Violent
- Disconnected from the divine
- Driven by ego

Murder was not an accident; it was the first fruit of a creation based on domination.

Why Was Murder the First Act?

Because the Second Creation was born from:

- Hierarchy
- Jealousy
- Fear
- Insecurity

Murder is the natural outcome of a lineage disconnected from spiritual unity.

Why Did the LORD God Protect Him?

The LORD God marks Cain because:

- Cain is part of his creation.
- Cain is his instrument.
- Cain will spread his influence.

This "mark" is not a curse—it is protection from beings Cain could not overpower.

Who Were the People in Nod?

The First Creation:

- Spiritually advanced
- Nonviolent
- Intuitive
- Living outside the LORD God's dominion
- Not subject to Eden's rules

This explains why they do not kill Cain. Violence is not in their nature.

How Cain Changed the World Through Mingling

When Cain mixes with the First Creation, humanity is forever altered:

- Spiritual DNA is diluted.
- Consciousness becomes divided.
- Conflict enters the human story.
- Domination spreads.

This is the birth of the world as we know it—a world ruled not by unity but by hierarchy.

Spiritual and Cultural Evidence of a Counterfeit Creator

Across Africa and the ancient world, civilizations preserved warnings about a false creator.

Dogon teachings describe:

- A demiurge-like being who miscreated humanity
- A shadow force jealous of the original beings

Gnostic texts reveal:

- A lesser god who claimed to be the only god
- A being who created a flawed physical world

Kemet teachings speak of:

- A chaotic force trying to imitate divine order

Mesopotamian myths describe:

- A craftsman god building physical bodies
- Using clay to trap the spirit

These cultures never lost the memory of a two-creation story.

Psychological Patterns of the Second Creation

Why does this second lineage fear the first?

Because the First Creation cannot be indoctrinated.
Spiritual intuition weakens control.
Because the First Creation retains ancestral memory.
Truth is a threat to systems built on deception.
Because the First Creation vibrates at a higher frequency.
Lower energies cannot dominate higher ones without suppression.
Because the First Creation is resilient.
Centuries of trauma could not erase their spiritual identity.
Because the First Creation carries prophecy.
Their awakening signals the end of the counterfeit.

Why Black People Are Feared—Not Hated

The world does not fear what is weak.
The world fears what is divine.

Spiritual Reasons

Melanated people are:

- Naturally intuitive
- Spiritually attuned
- Able to access higher consciousness
- Connected to ancient memory

Genetic Reasons

Melanin carries:

- Electrical conductivity
- Heightened sensory perception.
- Deeper spiritual resonance

These traits signal divine origin.

Historical Reasons

- Every empire dominated Black people to prevent their rise.

Energetic Reasons

- The energy of the First Creation destabilizes deceptive systems.

Prophetic Reasons

Every ancient prophecy points to:

- A return of the first people
- A mass awakening
- The collapse of false kingdoms

This is why oppression is global, coordinated, and relentless.

What Happens When the First Creation Awakens

When the First Creation remembers who they are:

- Systems collapse.
- Deception loses power.
- Unity consciousness rises.
- Truth dismantles falsehood.
- The spiritual order returns.

The Second Creation's dominion depends on secrecy. History has been rewritten, scriptures rearranged, and truth buried to keep one thing hidden. The First Creation was never meant to be ruled. The Second Creation was never meant to lead. And the moment the original people awaken, the deception unravels. To understand how deep manipulation goes, you must confront the one symbol the world taught you to fear—the serpent.

- Not as a corrupter
- Not as a deceiver

But as the guardian of forbidden knowledge. They taught the world to fear the serpent because it was the only one capable of setting you free.

Plate III — Serpent

Chapter 3
The Serpent

The Serpent—The True Liberator

From the moment the Eden narrative was taken over by the physical god's followers, humanity was taught to fear the very being who came to set it free. The Serpent has long been cast as the villain, the deceiver, the force that led humanity into ruin. Yet when the story is read through the lens of two Gods—the spiritual Creator, Elohim, and the physical god, YHWH—the Serpent takes on a different identity altogether.

The Serpent was never the enemy. It was the messenger of the Higher God, the liberator of consciousness in a garden built on obedience and control.

Reframing Eden Through the Two-Gods Lens

The Garden of Eden was crafted by the physical god, the one who shaped bodies out of dust and ruled through restriction. It was this god—not Elohim—who placed the Tree of Knowledge in the garden and then forbade humanity from touching it. Only a ruler driven by fear of awakening would plant wisdom in plain sight and then threaten death to anyone who sought it. Elohim—the God of spirit, truth, and consciousness—would never forbid the expansion of awareness. The spiritual God creates through light, knowledge, and freedom. Whereas the physical god, YHWH—called the Demiurge in Gnostic writings—creates through hierarchy, command, and limitation. The voice that said, "Thou shalt not eat of it" was not the voice of Elohim. It was the voice of a lesser creator afraid of losing dominion.

The Serpent appears not as an enemy of God, but as the emissary of the true God, the one who wanted humanity awakened. The Serpent's message aligned perfectly with the nature of Elohim. This is why the Serpent encouraged Eve to seek wisdom—because Elohim's intention for humanity was growth, not blindness.

KJV Evidence Supporting the Serpent's Message

Even the King James Bible clues that reveal the serpent did not lie:

1. Eve does become wise. Genesis 3:6 (KJV)—"And when the woman saw that the tree was... to be desired to make one wise..." She saw exactly what the serpent said would happen.

2. Their eyes were opened. Genesis 3:7 (KJV)—"And the eyes of them both were opened…" Again, exactly as the serpent promised.
3. They did not die that day. YHWH says they would die "in the day" they ate the fruit, but they lived for hundreds of years.
4. God confirms the serpent's words. Genesis 3:22 (KJV)—"Behold, the man is become as one of us, to know good and evil." This is the most devastating proof: YHWH admits the Serpent told the truth.

These verses unveil the uncomfortable truth: The Serpent's message aligned with reality. The prohibition aligned with fear.

Why the Serpent Was Demonized

Once patriarchal systems seized spiritual authority, the Serpent had to be destroyed symbolically. Not because it was evil, but because it represented knowledge, and knowledge is the enemy of control. Empires cannot rule people who know who they are. They cannot dominate a woman who knows her divine place in creation. So, they rewrote the Serpent from liberator to villain and transformed Eve from prophetess to problem.

To control humanity, the feminine had to be diminished. To diminish the feminine, the Serpent had to be feared. To fear the Serpent, knowledge had to be demonized. Knowledge controlled is power controlled.

Eve as the First Liberator and Prophet

Eve was not deceived. She was awakened. She was the first to see beyond the illusion, the first to question the voice of command, the first to reach for a higher understanding. She was the mother of biological life, yes, but she was also the mother of spiritual consciousness. Eve became the first prophet because she refused to live in the dark. She chose truth over obedience, awakening over comfort, enlightenment over captivity. This is the foundation of the hidden war for power. If the woman is silenced, the world is silenced. If the woman is awakened, the world awakens. This is why the Serpent approached her—not because she was weak, but because she was ready. Her intuition was already attuned to the frequency of Elohim.

In Gnostic tradition, Eve is *honored* as the one who recognized the truth amid deception. The Serpent is portrayed as the divine messenger of the true God, while the one forbidding knowledge is exposed as the archon, the counterfeit creator.

Ancient Cultures and the Positive Serpent

Colonized religion may have painted the Serpent as evil, but ancient spiritual systems remembered its true role.

Kemet (Egypt)

- The Uraeus serpent worn on the pharaoh's forehead symbolized protection, wisdom, and divine authority.
- Wadjet, the Serpent goddess, guarded truth and spiritual power.

India

- Kundalini is depicted as a coiled serpent rising through the chakras, awakening enlightenment.

Dogon of Mali

- Nommo beings are linked with water, wisdom, transformation, and symbolism.

Native American Traditions

- Carried serpentine. The Serpent represents rebirth, the cycles of nature, and the flow of cosmic energy.

Maya/Aztec

- Quetzalcoatl, the feathered serpent, brought knowledge and civilization. These cultures didn't demonize the serpent—they honored it.

The Serpent as Spiritual Energy and Human Awakening

The Serpent is a symbol encoded into the human body:

- DNA coils like a serpent (double helix).
- Kundalini energy rises up the spine like a serpent.
- The pineal gland—the seat of spiritual sight—is often represented by a serpent.
- Serpents shed their skin, symbolizing rebirth and evolution.

The Serpent in Eden was never meant to be literal. It was the symbol of awakening energy, the force that rises to restore spiritual sight.

How Eden the Story Became a Tool of Control

When patriarchy and empire joined forces, Eden became a doctrine of fear. By framing knowledge as sin, humanity became dependent on priests. By blaming the woman, society justified silencing her voice. By demonizing the serpent, spiritual awakening could be suppressed. By rewriting the fall, people were taught to feel unworthy.

People who feel sinful are easy to control. People who feel divine are impossible to enslave. The Serpent threatened the entire system—not because it brought death, but because it brought freedom.

The Awakening Begins

When the Serpent opened humanity's eyes, the illusion collapsed.

Eve carried the awakening.

Adam received it through her.

And that knowledge began to spread.

Humanity started rising in consciousness.

Light began to return to the world.

And the counterfeit creator panicked.

His next move was global.

It was calculated.

And it changed the trajectory of human civilization.

To stop humanity from awakening together, the physical god launched a new strategy:

- Confusion
- Division
- Scattering

What came next was the most dramatic attempt to crush human unity in history.

The story turns next to the Tower of Babel.

Plate IV — Tower of Babel

Chapter 4
The Tower of Babel

FOR GENERATIONS, CHURCHES HAVE REPEATED THE SAME shallow explanation: the Tower of Babel was about "human pride," and the people were punished for trying to "become gods." Yet when we read the King James Version with awakened eyes—eyes freed from the conditioning of colonized religion—a different revelation emerges. A revelation hidden in plain sight.

The Bible begins the story with a powerful truth. Genesis 11:1 (KJV)—"And the whole earth was of one language, and of one speech." This was not merely about vocabulary. This was oneness of consciousness, oneness of vibration, oneness of spiritual frequency. Humanity was living in harmony—not divided by race, doctrine, nation, or hierarchy. It was the remnant memory of the first creation, the children still carrying the vibration of Elohim, the spiritual Creator of unity, truth, and divine intelligence.

In that unity, something extraordinary began to happen. The people started building—not a building of pride, but a symbol of spiritual ascent. Genesis 11:4 (KJV)—"And they said… let us build us a city and a tower, whose top may reach unto heaven." They were rising back toward the realm they came from.

They remembered who they were.

They were returning to the divine frequency.

Then comes the verse that exposes the true nature of the "LORD" who steps into this narrative. Genesis 11:5 (KJV)—"And the LORD came down to see the city and the tower…"

Pause here.

Why would an all-knowing, spiritual Creator need to "come down" to see anything?

Elohim, the spiritual God of Genesis 1, does not "come down." Elohim speaks, breathes, and creation manifests.

But the one who comes down here behaves differently, watching nervously as humanity rises in unity.

Then the most revealing sentence in the entire story is spoken. Genesis 11:6 (KJV)—"Behold, the people is one… and now nothing will be restrained from them, which they have imagined to do."

This is the confession of a fearful god, not a loving Creator.

A true divine Being does not fear human unity.

A counterfeit one does.

Paul later confirms the existence of this deceptive being. 2 Corinthians 4:4 (KJV)—"The god of this world hath blinded the minds of them which believe not." This "god of this world"—the imitator, the demiurge, the architect of limitation—is the same voice that descends at Babel.

It is the same presence that placed restrictions in Eden. Now, this same entity is terrified that humanity might awaken to its divine power.

And what does this entity do in response to human unity? Genesis 11:7 (KJV)—"Go to, let us go down, and there confound their language, that they may not understand one another's speech."

Confusion was not punishment.

It was prevention.

Separation was not judgment.

It was control.

Language was not divided for humility. It was divided to stop humanity from remembering their origin in Elohim. Genesis 11:8 (KJV) says—"So the Lord scattered them abroad from thence upon the face of all the earth." This echoes the greatest trauma in the story of Black people.

- Scattering
- Displacement
- Broken languages
- Broken tribes
- Broken memories

This is not a coincidence. This is a pattern.

Just as the people of Babel were separated so they could not unite in power, Black people were scattered across continents through colonization, enslavement, and spiritual theft. Our languages were forbidden, our names erased, our spiritual systems demonized, and our unity violently torn apart.

The Imitator God Knows

People who speak the same spiritual language can rise.

People who walk in unity can ascend.

People who remember their origin become unstoppable.

This is why YHWH—the physical god, the god of limitation—confounded Babel. Global powers later repeated that same strategy against us.

The Hidden Revelation Inside the KJV

The Bible itself reveals the deception if we dare to read what it actually says.

- Humanity did not sin in this story.
- Humanity was united.
- Humanity did not rebel.
- Humanity rose together.

The text never says Elohim was displeased. The displeasure comes only from the "LORD" who comes down, limits, confuses, and scatters.

A God of Love does not fear human imagination.

A God of Truth does not silence unity.

A God of Spirit does not break what He created.

Babel was not the fall of man. It was the fall of the counterfeit god's control.

The imitator confesses with its own words. Genesis 11:6 (KJV)—"Nothing will be restrained from them." This was the *fear* of humanity remembering its divinity.

Reclaiming Babel: The Return of Unity

We stand today in the same spiritual moment. Black unity is not political. It is prophetic. It is divine. It is the return to what was stolen. When we align spiritually, economically, mentally, and physically, we rebuild the tower—not of brick and mortar, but of consciousness.

We rebuild with truth.

We rebuild with remembrance.

We rebuild with the frequency of Elohim

Our unity is the tower.

Our awakening is the ascent.

Our harmony is the path.

The powers of the world fear a rising people because a united, awakened people shatter the deception of the "god of this world" and expose the architect behind centuries of spiritual blindness.

The Tower Was Never a Threat to the Creator—Only to the Deceiver

The scattering at Babel was not divine judgment. It was divine sabotage by the imitator who knew his time was short. Once humanity awakens—once unity returns—the false kingdom collapses. And that collapse brings us to the next revelation—the next shadow lurking behind the story. The next power operating behind confusion, deception, and control.

The Bible calls him by many names: the accuser, the deceiver, the scripture-twister, the opposer.

But who is he really?

Where did he come from?

And why is he obsessed with keeping humanity blind?

As the imitator scatters bodies, this being scatters minds.

As the counterfeit god confuses tongues, this being confuses truth.

As the lesser LORD controls the physical world, this one seeks to rule the inner world.

Now, with the truth of Babel exposed, we step into the next chapter.

PART TWO

Who Really Rules the World?

Plate V — Satan

Chapter 5
Satan

People say they believe in God all the time. My question is, *What God do you believe in?*

Who Is the God of This World?

Before we can speak about Satan's plan, YHWH's identity, or how the white man fits into the physical world order, we must start with the question the Bible itself warns us about—the question most readers never ask: Who is the god of this world? The apostle Paul answers with unsettling clarity in 2nd Corinthians.

2 Corinthians 4:4 (KJV)—"In whom the god of this world hath blinded the minds of them which believe not."

Stop right there.

Paul did not say Elohim.

He did not say the Father of spirits.

He did not say the Most High God of creation.

Paul said there is a god of THIS world—a being who blinds human minds, blocks spiritual awakening, and hides the true light of Christ (the spiritual Christ, not the physical one invented by the system). This being rules this physical realm—the realm of flesh, fear, deception, violence, nations, politics, warfare, ego, and control.

Paul is not speaking symbolically. The Gospels agree. Lest the light of the glorious gospel of Christ, who is the image of God, should shine unto them. See, in the Bible we are told that Satan is the God of this world.

We see this in Matthew 4:8-9 (KJV)—"Again the Devil taketh Jesus up on an exceeding high mountain, and sheweth Him all the kingdoms of the world, and the glory of them; And saith unto him, All these things will I give thee, if thou wilt fall down and worship me." No god could offer what he does not own.

This is the first clue: If Satan could offer every kingdom, then every kingdom belongs to him—not to Jesus.

So again:

Who is the god of this world?

The Bible calls him Satan.

Yet when we look deeper into the Old Testament—and remove the conditioning—another truth emerges: The god of this world behaves exactly like YHWH.

YHWH and Satan: Two Names, One Character

The Old Testament "LORD" (YHWH) displays the very same behaviors attributed to Satan in the New Testament.

1. Both Blind Minds

- Satan blinds minds (2 Cor. 4:4).
- YHWH blinds eyes and hearts.
- Isaiah 6:10—"Make the heart of this people fat… shut their eyes; lest they see…" The same method.

4. Both Deceive

- Satan is the deceiver of the whole world (Rev. 12:9).
- But so is YHWH.

1 Kings 22:23 (KJV)—"The LORD hath put a lying spirit in the mouth of all these thy prophets…"

Ezekiel 14:9 (KJV)—"If the prophet be deceived… I the LORD have deceived that prophet…"

4. Both Test, Accuse, and Punish

- Satan tests Job—destroys his family.
- YHWH tests Abraham—demands the sacrifice of his son.
- Both demand suffering.
- Both demand fear.
- Both demand obedience under threat.

5. Both Promote Death and Destruction

Satan is called "a murderer from the beginning." YHWH orders genocide.

- Deuteronomy 20:16–17
- Joshua 6:21
- 1 Samuel 15:3

Both act as destroyers.

6. Both Demand Worship

Satan demands worship in exchange for power (Matt. 4:9). YHWH demands exclusive worship under threat (Exodus 20:5). These are not the ways of Elohim—the spiritual Creator who breathed life. These are the ways a being rules a physical domain:

- Fear
- Deception
- War
- Sacrifice
- Punishment
- Bloodshed

Thus, the unapologetic conclusion: The Old Testament "LORD" (YHWH) and Satan share the same identity— the god of this physical world, not the God of Spirit. Christ states, "the prince of this world cometh…" (John 14:30). Christ is not describing Himself, nor Elohim—He is describing the same entity Paul calls "the god of this world."

The Final Revelation

Christ exposes that:

- YHWH is tied to the physical realm.
- YHWH operates through fear, control, and obedience.
- YHWH blinds, limits, and restricts knowledge.
- YHWH governs the outer kingdom.

While Christ reveals that:

- The inner kingdom is within.
- The mind is freed instead of bound.

- Vision is restored instead of blinded.
- The path leads to Elohim, the spiritual Creator.

Christ doesn't destroy YHWH. Christ exposes YHWH by embodying a truth that YHWH cannot imitate: love, light, freedom, and universal spirit.

* * *

How Satan/YHWH Uses the White Man as His Physical Instrument

Just as Christ is the visible image of Elohim in Spirit, Satan/YHWH uses a visible image of himself in the physical world—not Satan incarnate, but a vehicle, a chosen instrument for the physical rule of the god of this world.

The White Man as the Tool of Physical Dominion

I'm not calling the white man Satan—I am just identifying the role.

Satan is a spirit. YHWH is the ruler of the physical realm. Both operate through a physical host civilization, just as Elohim operates spiritually through His chosen people.

The Bible shows this pattern:

- Pharaoh was used to oppress Israel.
- Rome was used to crucify Christ.
- Babylon was used to enslave Judah.

World powers are the instruments of the god of this world. Now, if we look at history, which group of people:

- Conquered continents?
- Erased nations?

- Rewrote the Bible?
- Redrew maps?
- Created caste systems?
- Built global empires of domination?
- Controlled media, education, religion, and finance?
- Spread their image as the "ideal human"?
- Erased the spiritual heritage of Black people?

Only one, and they did it globally, with the same strategic, emotionless precision seen in YHWH's dealings in the Old Testament.

This is not a coincidence.

This is an order.

This is an assignment.

This is lineage

The white man became the physical extension of YHWH/Satan's dominion over Earth. Not because of race superiority—but because the god of this world needed:

- A creation aligned with conquest
- A civilization tuned to domination
- People conditioned to expansion and control
- And a mindset built on hierarchy and rulership

The white man is the agent, not the architect.

Satan/YHWH is the architect.

The Black man is the target.

Elohim is the true Creator.

Plate VI — Two Versions of Jesus

Chapter 6
Two Versions of Jesus— The Flesh vs. the Spirit

THERE IS A MYSTERY BURIED DEEP WITHIN THE BIBLE—ONE that challenges centuries of religious teaching and demands that we think beyond the surface. Could it be that Jesus was never meant to be understood as a physical man, but as a divine energy, a spiritual messenger, a force of truth that transcends flesh and blood? The Jesus we've been taught to worship in church—a man who came to fulfill the Law of Moses—might not reflect the original, higher truth. Instead, Jesus came to fulfill something deeper: the spiritual blueprint buried beneath the law—a divine path meant to awaken the soul, not bind the body.

The Mosaic Law, with its rituals, sacrifices, and rigid commandments, was never the ultimate expression of God's will. Instead, it was part of a lower order—a flesh-based system rooted in control. The Apostle Paul acknowledges this when he writes, "For the law made nothing perfect, but the bringing in of a better hope did; by the which we draw nigh unto God." (Hebrews 7:19 KJV).

That "better hope" was not about stricter obedience—it was about spiritual awakening. Jesus did not come to play by the rules of the old priesthood. He came to dismantle it entirely.

Paul further states, "For there is verily a disannulling of the commandment going before for the weakness and unprofitableness thereof." (Hebrews 7:18 KJV).

Why was the law weak? Because it was earthly, rooted in temporary things like bloodlines, sacrifices, and outward purity. It bound people to performance and external rituals. But Jesus, like Melchizedek, came to reintroduce something eternal: the divine law of the Spirit, which predates sin, nations, and flesh.

Early Gnostic Christians believed Jesus was never meant to be viewed as a flesh-and-blood man who died to satisfy an angry god. Instead, he was understood as divine wisdom incarnate, the Light of the true Source, sent to liberate souls trapped in the illusion of the material world. He didn't come to save us from our humanity. He came to remind us of our divinity. According to the Gnostics, the material world was crafted by a lesser god, a false creator known as the Demiurge—a being who claimed to be the Most High but was blind and arrogant. This Demiurge created laws, systems, and religious rituals to keep humanity in ignorance and obedience.

In that false system, the Law of Moses became a tool of bondage. Yet Jesus came to shatter that illusion. The writer of Hebrews describes Jesus as a priest "not after the law of a carnal commandment, but after the power of an endless life." (Hebrews 7:16 KJV). Jesus did not come to fix the Law—He came to replace it. He offered a new covenant, not rooted in flesh, but in Spirit. This is how He truly "fulfilled" the law—not by obeying every rule or being a physical sacrifice, but by transcending the Law and revealing a better way:

The law of Spirit. The law of Light. The law of Love. The law of inner knowing. The veil in the temple was torn. The sacrifices ended. The outer temple fell so that the inner temple—your spirit—could rise.

The order of Melchizedek calls us inward to remember who we are. So, where did the idea of a physical Jesus come from?

Mainstream Christianity tells us that Jesus was a literal man, born of a virgin, descended from David, came to die as a sacrifice, and fulfilled the Mosaic Law. But what if that narrative was part of the lower system—the very system Jesus came to liberate us from? What if the "Jesus" that the church created was a manufactured image designed to keep people tied to the Old Covenant—a system of blood, hierarchy, and submission?

The Bible says that Jesus came "after the order of Melchizedek" (Psalm 110:4; Hebrews 5:6). But who was Melchizedek? Hebrews 7:3 tells us he was "without father, without mother, without descent, having neither beginning of days, nor end of life; but made like unto the Son of God…" In other words, he was an eternal being, not defined by physical lineage. This points to something beyond flesh. If Jesus came in that same order, then Jesus, too, is best understood not as a man born of a woman, but as a divine, timeless force. Yet for centuries, Christianity has insisted on a version of Jesus rooted in the flesh—a man descended from David, tied to the God of the Old Testament, YHWH.

This version was built on the idea that Jesus fulfilled YHWH's covenant with David (see 2 Samuel 7:12–16). However, few stop to ask: Who is YHWH?

The Bible describes YHWH as a "jealous God" (Exodus 20:5, KJV), a god of wrath, war, and sacrifice. Gnostic writings suggest that YHWH may be the Demiurge—the false god who imposed a lower law to keep people bound. If that's the case, then Jesus, as presented by the church, may not be a liberator at all, but a trap. Even the name "Jesus" comes from the Hebrew Yehoshua, meaning "YHWH saves." If YHWH is not the true Most High—not El Elyon—then what kind of salvation are we being offered? Obedience, fear, submission?

This is the great spiritual deception: they wrapped divine truth in human skin, created a flesh-and-blood Jesus, and told us to worship Him instead of becoming Him. They said, "Bow to Jesus, and you'll be saved by YHWH," but in truth, they were leading us back into spiritual bondage. The real Christ, the one the Gnostics knew, did not point people to YHWH.

He pointed them inward. Luke 17:21 (KJV)—"The kingdom of God is within you."

"Ye are gods." (John 10:34, quoting Psalm 82:6 KJV).

This Jesus—this divine teacher—was not establishing a religion. He was revealing your divine nature. He came to dismantle religious hierarchy, not to build it up. He came to make priests of all people, not to hand power to a chosen few.

So, what happened?

The church took this spiritual teacher, the one full of truth and light, and buried His message under layers of tradition and control. They connected Him to the lineage of David, claimed He fulfilled YHWH's promise, and made Him the poster child for sacrifice. They ignored that Melchizedek—and by extension, the true Christ—had no earthly lineage at all. He represented the Most High God— El Elyon, not YHWH. He existed before Israel, before law, before flesh.

The Christ they don't want you to know is not a man to worship—but still, people are told to wait for Jesus to return from the clouds, as if salvation is coming from outside. Jesus Himself warned against this kind of thinking:

Matthew 24:23 (KJV)—"Then if any man shall say unto you, Lo, here is Christ, or there; believe it not."

Matthew 24:26 (KJV)—"Behold, he is in the desert; go not forth: behold, he is in the secret chambers; believe it not."

Why?

Because the return of Christ is not external—it is internal. It is the awakening of divine consciousness within each of us. Every time someone breaks free from fear, shame, and religious programming, Christ returns. Every time someone remembers their divine identity, the second coming begins.

Even the title "Morning Star" carries a mystery. In Revelation 22:16, Jesus says, "I am the root and the offspring of David, and the bright and morning star."

In Isaiah 14:12, that same image is used—the one who fell, a king who exalted himself and was brought low.

Religion later called this "Lucifer" and turned him into the devil. The truth is deeper: Morning Star is not a person but a symbol—the bearer of light. In one story, misused light leads to a fall; in the other, revealed light leads to awakening. Both point us to the same lesson: rise beyond the ego, awaken, and return to the Christ consciousness.

You were never meant to be ruled by fear.

You were never meant to wait for salvation.

You are not here to worship Christ.

You are here to become Christ.

Plate VII — Suppression

Chapter 7

The Suppression

Engines of Erasure

From the Roman to the British Empire, these were not mere governments—they were machines of cultural theft and genocidal conquest. The knowledge of the Black man is rooted in Alkebulan—the name of Africa before the white man changed it—a word meaning "mother of mankind" or "Garden of Eden." In Kemet, which is modern-day Egypt, Nubia, Mali, and Ethiopia were seen as a threat to white supremacy. So, it was stolen, twisted, and claimed as their own.

The rise of white power was never about civilization—it was about subjugation. It was about silencing the truth that the builders of pyramids, the keepers of the stars, and the stewards of sacred geometry were Black. Here are several more historical empires that acted as "engines of erasure," each systematically looting Black knowledge, culture, and sovereignty to reinforce white supremacy.

From the 15th to the 20th centuries, the Portuguese Empire sent explorers into West Africa who stole manuscripts, oral histories, and sacred artifacts from kingdoms like Benin and the Kongo. They pioneered the Atlantic slave trade, uprooting millions of West and Central Africans from their lands and severing lines of ancestral transmission. Catholic missionaries destroyed indigenous shrines and replaced them with European churches, rebranding local cosmologies as "pagan" to be stamped out.

From the 15th to the 19th centuries, the Spanish Empire expanded into parts of North and West Africa. They looted African libraries, brought back gold and ivory, and codified African religious cosmologies as witchcraft. The encomienda system in Spanish-controlled territories forced Black labor on plantations and in mines under brutal conditions, decimating entire communities.

The Spanish colonial law banned the teaching of indigenous languages and the practice of their ceremonies, criminalizing the transmission of African knowledge. Then we have the Ottoman Empire from the 14th to the 20th centuries. Where the Ottomans absorbed Ethiopian and Nubian manuscripts into their imperial libraries, they obscured their African origin by cataloguing them under the Ottoman calligraphy schools. The Ottoman insurrection laws outlawed the teaching of indigenous African Sufi orders, pushing their practices underground.

From the 17th to the 20th centuries, the French Colonial Empire expanded across West and Central Africa. French ethnographers and archaeologists expropriated art and artifacts from kingdoms such as Dahomey and the Mali Empire, shipping these treasures back to Paris museums. The policy of assimilation forced African elites to adopt the French language and customs; children were sent to "écoles de mission," mission schools run by Christian clergy, where they were severed from their families and traditions.

Then we have the Belgian Congo from 1885 to around 1960. Under King Leopold II, Congolese art, sacred objects, and even human remains were harvested for European museums and scientific exhibits.

Colonial administrators banned local religious ceremonies and kinship practices, replacing them with Catholic sacraments and European social structures.

Then we also have the Dutch Empire from the 17th to the 20th centuries. The Dutch East India Company and West India Company seized African manuscripts, botanical knowledge, and metallurgical techniques from the Kingdom of Loango and the Ashanti Empire. The Dutch Reformed missionaries obliterated indigenous spiritual sites, constructing churches atop former shrines to assert spiritual conquest.

How We Became Suppressed Through Religion

Missionaries of Agents of Empire

European missionaries would often arrive before soldiers. Under the banner of "saving souls," they laid the foundation for colonization by undermining indigenous spirituality. In places like Zimbabwe and Ghana, traditional priests were labeled "witch doctors," sacred groves were burned, and indigenous cosmologies were declared demonic. Missionaries elevated certain tribes over others, converting select groups and using them as long-standing divisions that still exist today. From the stained-glass windows to children's Bibles, Jesus, angels, and prophets were portrayed as white Europeans.

Reprogramming Black People to Subconsciously Associate Holiness with Whiteness

By repeatedly presenting divinity in white form, churches rewired generations of Black believers to view their features, color, and culture as inferior or sinful. During slavery, Black people were allowed to gather for church, but only under white oversight, and only to hear verses like "Servants, obey your masters."

Black preachers were often selected or monitored by slaveholders to ensure they promoted obedience, not liberation. Those who preached messages of freedom risked brutal punishment or death. Even after slavery, many Black churches were modeled after the structure of white institutions, hierarchical, patriarchal, and disconnected from their African spiritual roots. Systems like Vodun and Candomblé—rich spiritual paths from West Africa—were cast as witchcraft or satanic by Christian missionaries and colonizers. In places such as Haiti, Brazil, and the United States, practicing ancestral religions could lead to imprisonment or lynching. The wisdom of drumming, trance, spirit possession, herbal medicine, and ancestral reverence was stripped away and replaced with pews, pulpits, and passive worship.

Many major Christian denominations—Anglican, Baptist, and Catholic—owned slaves, profited from the trade, and preached theology that upheld it. These same churches funded missionary schools that taught Black children European values while erasing their cultural identity. To this day, most churches have not repented for these crimes in any meaningful way. Some even still display whitewashed images of the divine without question. Now the awakening is returning. The drum beats again.

Dreams carry messages. Ancestors whisper. The original creation remembers who it is, not a servant, but a divine being made in the Creator's image. Beneath the surface of governments, religions, and institutions lies a far more elusive force: the shadow elite. Or should we say secret societies? These are not just politicians or preachers. They are secret architects. Planners. Puppeteers. Their reach extends across continents, into boardrooms, war rooms, and seminaries. Although they appear to be many, their motives are unified: to maintain control over the collective mind, especially that of the Black man. The irony is this: many of these secret societies trace their power not to Europe but to Africa.

The Freemasons, for instance, study sacred geometry, the symbolism of the pyramids, solar worship, and the principles of balance deeply rooted in the mystery systems of Kemet or Ancient Egypt. The Illuminati, originally born in Europe as a rebellion against the church's ignorance, absorbed knowledge from Moorish scholars and African texts during the so-called "Dark Ages," when Africa held the knowledge, and Europe wandered in superstition. Rather than honoring these truths, these societies weaponized what was sacred. The mysteries were locked away. Symbols like the Eye of Horus, the Ankh, and sacred numerology were rebranded under the cloak of occult secrecy—disconnected from their African origins.

They operate under creeds of secrecy and symbolism, often swearing oaths that supersede national or religious loyalties. Their true allegiance is to order and control through hierarchy. Not divine order, but artificial dominion. The hidden powers don't need armies on the ground. They control through media propaganda. The mainstream news is shaped by corporate and political interests, filtering truth and framing narratives that favor global elites. Entertainment is used to glorify violence, sexualize youth, and drown out spiritual awakening with noise.

They create false crises. Wars, pandemics, and social upheavals are sometimes sparked or exploited to justify new laws, surveillance, and restrictions. The Federal Reserve, IMF, and World Bank are tools of debt enslavement, keeping nations and people in bondage while pretending to offer aid. When any group—especially Black movements—begin to rise with truth, they are infiltrated, discredited, or destroyed from within. These societies know something that most don't. The original Black man is not just physical; he is metaphysical. His melanin, his intuition, his ancestral connection, his dream life, his rhythm, and his spiritual power are all considered a threat. So, the white man's mission is clear:

Keep the Black man distracted.
Keep the Black woman disempowered.
Keep the Black child miseducated.
Keep the ancient knowledge buried.

Plate VIII — Secret History

Chapter 8
A Secret History

THE STORY OF SUPPRESSION IS NOT JUST HISTORICAL. IT IS spiritual. It is psychological. And it is intentional. Those who rule this world aligned with YHWH's system have used suffering as a tool, a test, and a trap. However, this method of control is not new. It is ancient, embedded deep in the earliest texts. One of the clearest revelations of this hidden system lies in a story many read but never truly see.

Job

- A man praised for the purity of his spirit
- A man untouched by rebellion
- A man honored by Elohim for simply walking in spiritual integrity

Yet he becomes the target of a cosmic agreement between YHWH and Satan.

Why?

To reveal the system that governs this world. A system that still governs us today.

The Book of Job opens with a description rarely given to any human in Scripture.

Job 1:8 (KJV)—"Hast thou considered my servant Job, that there is none like him in the earth, a perfect and an upright man...?" "Perfect" here does not mean without flaw in the flesh. It means perfect in spirit, aligned with Elohim—a being whose consciousness was pure, balanced, awake.

Job was already moving in what we would call Christ Consciousness—a state of unity, trust, and direct spiritual alignment. He was everything the system of YHWH and Satan feared. And so the test begins, but the test does not come from Elohim.

The Agreement They Made

Job 1:12 (KJV)—"And YHWH said unto Satan, Behold, all that he hath is in thy power..." reveals a disturbing truth: There is no argument between them.

- No conflict
- No war in heaven
- Just cooperation

YHWH gives Satan permission. Satan carries it out.

Elohim watches as a third party—without intervening. The story goes further.

After Job passes the first test, still refusing to curse Elohim, YHWH again brings Job into the conversation. Job 2:3 (KJV)—"...thou movedst me against him, to destroy him without cause." This shows YHWH admitting the truth: "Without cause"—meaning Job was innocent.

This is not the Creator testing His creation.

This is the system testing the spiritually awakened because the system seeks control, loyalty, and limitation.

This is the blueprint for every spiritual attack on awakened people.

This is the secret history.

The System of Suffering

Job suffers not because he sinned.

Because he was righteous.

Because he was awake.

Because he was aligned with Elohim rather than YHWH. YHWH and Satan work together to break him.

Why?

- To prove a point
- To maintain dominance
- To show that suffering can force a human back into submission

This same system rules our world today. A world where suffering is not accidental.

Where oppression is not random.

Where pain becomes the tool used to keep those with divine DNA asleep.

Job becomes the story of the awakened soul targeted by the false god.

Job's Awakening Through Suffering

Here is the part they never preach: The suffering did not destroy Job.

- It elevated him.
- It stripped away fear.
- It revealed the truth.
- It increased his spiritual capacity.

Job did not curse Elohim. He did not bow to the fear imposed by YHWH's tests. He did not surrender his spiritual identity.

Instead, Job awakened to a deeper spiritual awareness. He began to question the nature of suffering. He began to seek answers beyond the system. He began to look inward—awakening Christ Consciousness through endurance.

Job's awakening mirrors ours.

Are We Job?

Look at our world today.
We see:

- Suffering without cause
- Oppression that targets the innocent
- Systems built to test loyalty, not to grow the spirit
- Spiritual attacks that come from the very forces claiming to "protect"
- A world designed to break those aligned with truth

Just like Job, the awakened people of today are tested because they carry the spiritual spark of Elohim. We are targeted not because we are weak, but because we are powerful. Not because we are sinful, but because we are spiritually dangerous to the system.

The story of Job is our story.

- A people stripped
- A people broken down
- A people misjudged
- A people enduring cycles of spiritual attack

Yet in the end, a people restored with greater wisdom, vision, and spiritual authority. What they intended for destruction became the doorway to awakening.

Be Vigilant

Job's story is also a warning for the awakened soul.

The Bible tells us plainly:

1 Peter 5:8 (KJV)—"Be sober, be vigilant; because your adversary the devil, as a roaring lion, walketh about, seeking whom he may devour."

Not devouring flesh:

- Devouring spirit
- Devouring identity
- Devouring consciousness
- Devouring connection to Elohim

The system that tested Job is the same system that roams today. And the awakened must remain alert. Christ Consciousness is light. But the opposition is relentless.

Job—And Us

Job's story ends not with defeat but ascension.

He receives:

- Spiritual clarity
- Deeper connection
- Greater understanding
- Multiplied blessings

Why?

Because the test could not break what Elohim had placed within him. This is the message for us today: The suffering you endured was not a sign of divine anger.

It is evidence of your spiritual identity.

It is the pressure exerted by a lower system that seeks to break an awakened soul.

Like Job, *you cannot be broken.*

You are here to awaken.

To reclaim your power.

To rise beyond the system's reach.

Understanding Job helps us grasp the true nature of the system we face. Yet the story does not end with tests or suffering. The next step is to uncover how truth itself was flipped, reshaped, and reversed to keep us blind to our divine nature.

Plate IX — The Flip

Chapter 9
The Flip

MATTHEW 20:16 (KJV)—"SO THE LAST SHALL BE FIRST, and the first last: for many be called, but few chosen." For generations, talk of a New World Order has echoed across political halls, church pulpits, and conspiracy circles alike. It has been painted as a terrifying reign of power: centralized control, hidden rulers, and a loss of freedom.

Yet what if this fear, this anxiety about a New World Order, is rooted in a misunderstanding? What if the true shift is not the rise of new oppressors but the fall of the old ones? What if the New World being created is not an extension of the same systems of domination, but a divine reversal, long foretold?

Jesus Christ, speaking to His disciples, said plainly, "The last shall be first, and the first last" (Matthew 20:16 KJV). His words, though often quoted, are rarely understood in their full spiritual depth. In a world constructed on false hierarchies—economic, racial, and religious beliefs—His statement rings with a revolutionary frequency. In the context of this flipped, crumbling world, His words do not simply offer comfort; they proclaim a prophecy. A prophecy of restoration. A prophecy of truth emerging from beneath centuries of lies.

Who Are "The Last"?

To understand the weight of Jesus's words, we must first understand who "the last" truly is. In today's world, the answer is painfully clear. The last are the ones placed at the bottom of every fabricated hierarchy. The last are the ones who, despite being the foundation of human civilization, are treated as the least among men.

Black people—scattered through the horrors of slavery, colonialism, systemic racism, and economic sabotage—have lived the reality of being "the last" by design, not by nature. Stripped of their names, their lands, their gods, and their dignity, they were made to believe that they are nothing. Yet the Bible tells a different story. It proclaims the victory of those who suffer in righteousness:

Matthew 5:10 (KJV)—"Blessed are they which are persecuted for righteousness' sake: for theirs is the kingdom of heaven."

Black people's persecution has never been because of their inferiority but because of their innate greatness. It is because the blood of kings and priests flows through their veins. It is because they are closer to the divine origin, the creative breath of the Most High Himself. Their fall was orchestrated; their rise is ordained.

Likewise, we must identify "the first"—those who have placed themselves at the top of this inverted world. They are not first because God exalted them. They are first because they built systems—economic, religious, educational—that enshrined their illusion of superiority. They crafted lies, maintained them through violence, and called it civilization. They fulfilled the ancient warning of the prophet Isaiah:

Isaiah 5:20 (KJV)—"Woe unto them that call evil good, and good evil; that put darkness for light, and light for darkness."

Colonizers called their theft "discovery." Slaveholders called their wickedness "Christian duty." Oppressors called their rule "manifest destiny." *Yet the Most High sees all.* No lie can remain unchallenged forever. Those who have taken the seats of power through deceit are nearing the moment when they must step down—not by human revolution, but by divine reversal.

The Reversal of the Reversal

The world we inhabit today is already a reversal of truth. The divine has been demonized. The sacred has been desecrated. The righteous have been vilified. However, Jesus's words announce an even greater reversal: a restoration of what was stolen. When Christ says, "the last shall be first," He is not offering a vague hope for the afterlife. He is declaring a shift that begins even in this realm. The oppressed will rise—not only in spirit, but in power, in truth, and love.

Psalm 135:14 (KJV)—"For the Lord will judge his people, and he will repent himself concerning his servants."

Justice delayed is not justice denied. It is justice prepared.

Truth Is Buried, Not Lost

The oppressors have spent centuries rewriting history. They have whitewashed ancient greatness. They have twisted scripture to justify sin. They have buried sacred knowledge beneath layers of falsehood. Yet the truth has not been destroyed. It has merely been hidden.

Jesus Himself said: "For there is nothing covered, that shall not be revealed; neither hid, that shall not be known" (Luke 12:2 KJV).

The blood remembers. The bones remember. The spirit remembers. In rituals whispered in secret, in songs sung in sorrow, in dreams that defy logic, the truth has survived. Today, it stirs again. The descendants of the oppressed are remembering who they are—not through external validation, but through divine awakening.

The Call to Study and Resist

If we are to fulfill this prophecy, we must engage in intentional reclamation. Jesus commanded:

John 5:39 (KJV)—"Search the scriptures; for in them ye think ye have eternal life: and they are they which testify of me."

Studying is not just for scholars. It is a revolutionary act. Every hidden history we uncover, every suppressed text we read, every ancient practice we reclaim chips away at the structures of lies. We must resist the temptation to find comfort in systems never designed for our liberation. We must resist false religions that ask us to bow to images of our oppressors. We must resist economies that profit from our suffering. We must resist educational systems that erase our contributions.

Affirm Your Original Greatness

Resistance, however, is only the beginning. The deeper work is affirmation. We must proclaim, with holy boldness, our original greatness.

God said of His people: "Ye are the light of the world. A city that is set on a hill cannot be hid" (Matthew 5:14 KJV).

We are not cursed. We are blessed. We are not inferior. We are essential. We are not accidents. We are architects. Affirming our greatness is not arrogance. It is obedience to the truth. It is honoring the divine breath that animates our being. It is standing in the authority of the Most High, who said, "I have said, Ye are gods; and all of you are children of the most High." (Psalm 82:6 KJV).

Stop Worshipping Broken Systems

The old world is dying before our eyes. Systems built on exploitation and lies cannot sustain themselves forever. Revelation foretells this collapse:

Revelation 18:11 (KJV)—"And the merchants of the earth shall weep and mourn over her; for no man buyeth their merchandise any more."

Stop mourning the systems that enslaved you. Let them fall. Stop chasing seats at tables never meant for your nourishment. Build your own tables—rooted in divine truth, in communal power, in spiritual wisdom older than pyramids.

Isaiah 14:1–3 (KJV)—"For the LORD will have mercy on Jacob, and will yet choose Israel, and set them in their own land: and the strangers shall be joined with them, and they shall cleave to the house of Jacob. And the people shall take them, and bring them to their place: and the house of Israel shall possess them in the land of the LORD for servants and handmaids: and they shall take them captives, whose captives they were; and they shall rule over their oppressors. And it shall come to pass in the day that the LORD shall give thee rest from sorrow, and from thy fear, and from the hard bondage wherein thou wast made to serve."

Look into this chapter as a mirror and see yourself clearly: You are not cursed—you are blessed beyond measure. You are not lost—you are returning to your divine origin. You are not weak—you are the strength that carried generations through impossible storms.

The time of mourning is over. The time of remembering has come. The last are rising. The divine reversal is underway. Jesus's words are not ancient poetry. They are the architecture of the future. A future where the oppressed walk in power. A future where the first thrones built on lies crumble to dust. A future where truth reigns, and justice flows like a mighty river. Now we, as a people, must not forget what caused us to become in bondage and suffering, and why these things were allowed to happen to us—now, as we return to Reclamation.

PART THREE

The Path To Reclamation

Plate X — Power of Knowledge

Chapter 10
The Power of Knowledge

Isaiah 28:9–10 (KJV)—"Whom shall he teach knowledge? and whom shall he make to understand doctrine? them that are weaned from the milk, and drawn from the breasts. For precept must be upon precept, precept upon precept; line upon line, line upon line; here a little, and there a little."

Awakening Begins with the Word

To reclaim your power, you must first reclaim your mind—and nothing enslaves or frees the mind more than knowledge. The Bible, often misused and misunderstood, holds spiritual codes that have been intentionally hidden in plain sight. These verses were never meant to be read like a novel from cover to cover. They were designed as a divine puzzle, written "precept upon precept," requiring spiritual eyes and ears to decode.

When Isaiah says, "weaned from the milk," he's not talking about literal milk—he's talking about spiritual infancy. Too many people are still on the bottle of watered-down doctrines. They've been given only enough of the truth to keep them quiet, obedient, and asleep. It's like being given a child's version of a war manual—you'll never know how to fight if you're not given real weapons. Churches today are filled with surface-level teachings—emotional highs with no foundation. You hear "God loves you," but you're not taught how to access that power. You're told to wait for heaven, not to bring heaven to earth. This shallow gospel leaves you defenseless in a world ruled by deception.

Spiritual Literacy Was Stolen from Us

During slavery, reading the Bible was illegal for Black people. That wasn't just to keep them from learning letters—it was to keep them from discovering their lineage, their divinity, and their power. Enslavers cherry-picked verses like "Servants, obey your masters," while hiding verses like "Ye are gods; and all of you are children of the most High." (Psalm 82:6 KJV).

This wasn't ignorance; it was intentional miseducation. Still, that miseducation exists today. Many Black people were handed a colonized version of Christianity, the New Testament only stripped of its ancient African spiritual roots. They were taught to look outside of themselves for God, never within. But the kingdom is within you (Luke 17:21 KJV). The very power they sought to suppress has always been there, dormant, but not dead.

The Bible Is a Cipher—Not a Children's Storybook

To unlock the power of the Bible, you must read it as it was meant to be read: precept upon precept. That requires connecting verses across chapters, books, and even testaments to reveal hidden truths

Take these examples:

- Psalm 82:6—"Ye are gods…"
- Luke 17:21—"The kingdom of God is within you."
- John 10:34—"Jesus answered them, 'Is it not written in your law, I said, Ye are gods?'"

When these verses are linked together, a larger truth emerges. Divinity is not something you chase—it is something you awaken. But you must be taught how to see it. When you reclaim how to read scripture, you begin to see that the Bible doesn't belong to your oppressors.

It is not a white man's book. It is a Black ancestral text, filled with coded knowledge that has the power to dismantle false systems and ignite self-transformation. What was once used to chain the body can now free the soul.

This is why Hosea 4:6 hits hard: "My people are destroyed for lack of knowledge…" Not destroyed for lack of faith. Not destroyed for lack of prayer. *Because thou hast rejected knowledge.*

Now, there is a deeper, spiritual meaning behind the act of tithing that has been buried under centuries of religious tradition and misinterpretation.

The story of Abraham giving Melchizedek a tenth, or a tithe, is often cited as the foundational principle for financial tithing in modern churches. However, the true significance of this exchange is not about money; it is metaphysical. It speaks to the inner workings of the human mind and spirit.

Abraham, after returning victorious from battle, meets Melchizedek, described in Genesis 14 as the King of Salem and a priest of the Most High God. He gives Melchizedek a tenth of everything. Yet if we look more closely, we find that Melchizedek symbolizes divine wisdom and higher consciousness. He appears without explanation, with no recorded beginning or end, echoing the eternal nature of spiritual truth.

The act of Abraham giving a tenth to Melchizedek is not merely physical; it is deeply spiritual. This gesture represents giving 10 percent of our brain, the small fraction of consciousness we actively use, to God. Mainstream science tells us we only use about 10 percent of our brain's potential. When we devote this portion to focused meditation, prayer, and spiritual practice, we open ourselves to divine revelation. God then returns to us the remaining 90 percent, unlocking supernatural insight, wisdom, and the power to transcend the material world.

At this point, the churches have misled us. They've turned a spiritual principle into a financial obligation. They've taught us to give them 10 percent of our income under the guise of pleasing God. But this physical tithe was never meant to be the focus. It was always about the mind, the spirit, the consciousness. The requirement was never money, but intention, focus, and alignment with divine wisdom.

This misunderstanding has trapped generations in cycles of poverty and guilt, while robbing them of the essential truth. Jesus himself exposed this system. He taught us not to stand on street corners to pray or to perform rituals for show. Instead, he said,

Matthew 6:6 (KJV)—"But thou, when thou prayest, enter into thy closet, and when thou hast shut thy door, pray to thy Father which is in secret..."

This is a call to meditation, stillness, and divine communion. He taught silence over spectacle and solitude over ceremony. God is not found in noise, but in the quietness of the soul. Even more profound is Jesus's priesthood in the Order of Melchizedek. This order predates the Levitical priesthood that dominated Israel's religious system. The Levites operated under the Mosaic Law—rules, sacrifices, rituals—but Melchizedek's priesthood was not based on law.

It was based on eternal truth and divine presence. Hebrews 7 tells us that Jesus did not come from the tribe of Levi, yet He is a High Priest forever in the order of Melchizedek. This means that Jesus bypassed the religious system and the legalistic framework. He came with a higher authority, a greater wisdom. He came to fulfill the law, not by enforcing it, but by transcending it.

He came to show us that truth lies within, and that salvation is not found in external rituals but in inner transformation and divine connection. So, when we tithe our consciousness, when we give that focused 10 percent of our mind to God, we step into alignment with the Melchizedek order.

We reject the bondage of tradition and reclaim our spiritual authority. We awaken to the 90 percent that lies dormant within us, and we begin to operate not from fear and lack but from divine abundance, insight, and power.

Ignorance is not just a gap in understanding; it is a form of bondage. Hosea 4:6 doesn't speak of ignorance as a small issue but as the root cause of destruction. This isn't simply a matter of education, but of spiritual blindness, mental conditioning, and historical erasure. It's not what we don't know that keeps us enslaved; it's what we were never allowed to learn.

Black people across the globe have suffered not just physically but spiritually and mentally because our knowledge of self, origin, and power was deliberately hidden. We were not meant to remember because remembering our divinity would lead to reclamation. Reclamation threatens the entire structure of control.

Before any physical chains were placed on our ancestors, the first act of violence was mental. Names were stripped. Languages erased. Spiritual systems condemned. The African, once known as a king, queen, healer, prophet, and priest, was redefined as a savage, a heathen, and a slave. This spiritual identity theft was not a mistake. It was a calculated system of domination. When we were disconnected from our divine self-knowledge, we became programmable. Easily manipulated. Easily controlled.

What happens when gods forget who they are? They bow to idols. They chase validation from the very people who demonized them. They forget their power and seek approval from their oppressors. False knowledge is more dangerous than ignorance because it feels like the truth. When Black people were taught that Jesus was white, that heaven was beyond the clouds, and that submission was righteousness, they were not learning faith—they were learning fear.

Every time we accept lies about our past, our faith, and our worth, we unknowingly cooperate with our oppression. We didn't just forget. We were misled. Education in colonized systems didn't empower us; it programmed us. We learned to aspire to whiteness, to chase Western approval, and to equate intelligence with distance from Blackness. That is not knowledge. That is slavery of the mind.

Black children grow up in systems that teach them everything about Europe but nothing about Africa. They learn about Rome and Greece, but not about Timbuktu, Great Zimbabwe, or ancient Kush. The curriculum is designed to shape inferiority. This miseducation ensures that Black children grow into Black adults who question their worth. They doubt their greatness because they were never taught it. They believe their history started with chains, not crowns.

Like many, I once believed freedom meant achieving what they told me to achieve. Get the degree. Get a good job. Dress right. Talk right. But all it brought was emptiness. I wasn't walking in truth. I was walking in their programming.

Only when I began to question everything did the veil start to lift. I realized that my power wasn't in mimicking the white man; it was in rejecting it. It's about remembering who I was before the world told me who to be. This awakening is not unique to me. It's happening globally. More and more people are breaking the mental chains. That's why the truth is so dangerous. The truth is contagious. Now we must balance our energy—the Yin and Yang of the mind.

Plate XI — Waking Up with Love

Chapter 11
Waking Up with Love

THIS IS NOT A RACIAL BATTLE. IT IS A SPIRITUAL ONE, AND spiritual warfare is about energy. The war we are fighting is not between Black people and white people. That is the lie—the grand illusion, crafted by the architects of confusion.

We have been taught, generation after generation, to hate each other in the name of religion, in the name of nationalism, in the name of race—all while the real enemy hides behind the veil, untouched and empowered by our division.

- This is *not* a war of skin.
- This is a war of energy.
- This is a war of frequency.
- This is a war of truth versus manipulation, of divine light versus artificial illumination.

From birth, we've been programmed to believe that "Black" is evil, dark, dirty, or wicked, while "white" is pure, holy, and righteous. This twisted coding was not accidental. It was a ritual. A global spell. The reversal of truth itself. Many of us—both Black and white—have been unconscious participants in a system that feeds off of spiritual division. Let's be clear: Blackness is not a curse. It is not the absence of light—it is the womb of light. It is the origin of creation, the cosmic root, the eternal soil from which life emerges.

Black absorbs light not because it is void, but because it contains all frequencies within it. White, in an energetic sense, reflects and refracts. It blinds. It can dazzle. It can illuminate. When in the wrong hands, it becomes a tool of distortion—a mirror that hides instead of reveals.

This isn't about people. It's about the energetic meanings that have been weaponized against us all. We were not meant to be enemies. We were meant to be reflections of the True Creator in spirit. Sadly, the system taught the Black man to see himself as cursed. It taught the white man to see himself as God.

Both are lies. Both are prisons. So, how do we break free?

1. Change the Way We Think

Start with the language. Every time you associate Black with evil or inferior, pause and ask, "Where did I learn this? Whom does it serve?" Replace those thoughts with truth: Black is sacred. Black is foundational. Black is divine.

2. See Spirit, Not Skin

Look at people as energy, not flesh. Is their spirit aligned with the truth? With justice? With divine order? Or is it aligned with control, deception, and ego? Skin is a costume. Spirit is identity.

3. Reject the False God of Division

The god of this world thrives on conflict—racism, nationalism, and religious supremacy. Tear down those altars. Build new ones rooted in unity, compassion, and consciousness.

4. Return to Frequency—Meditate

Speak affirmations. Return to the Source. Raise your vibration through truth, discipline, and spiritual study. When your energy is high, deception loses its grip.

Positive energy builds, heals, and creates. Negative energy destroys, divides, and deceives. When you are kept in ignorance, you are more easily kept in fear—a state that weakens you. Knowledge brings light. Light brings balance. We must become whole. That means balancing the masculine and feminine, the logic and intuition, the physical and the spiritual. The system taught us to chase power externally. Real power is internal. It's in your energy. Your awareness. Your frequency. The greatest threat to the current world order is not protest. It's not even a revolution. It's awakening.

Unity In Spirit: One Energy, One People

Galatians 3:28 (KJV)—"There is neither Jew nor Greek, there is neither bond nor free, there is neither male nor female: for ye are all one in Christ Jesus."

Once the veil is lifted, we realize the war has never been about skin—it has always been about spirit. From the beginning, systems of power have used race, religion, gender, and class as tools to divide and conquer. Even so, beneath these surface identities lies a much deeper reality: we are one energy, one people, flowing from a divine source.

We are not physical beings reaching for spirit—we are spiritual beings enduring a physical illusion. That illusion becomes our prison when we forget who we are, when we believe in the labels, when we fight each other instead of the systems that keep us enslaved. The message of Galatians 3:28 breaks through the illusion: there is no separation in truth. The Creator did not design hierarchy; man did. When Jesus said in Matthew 22:39, "Love thy neighbor as thyself," He wasn't giving a simple moral suggestion. He was revealing a key to liberation.

Once we see each other as reflections of the divine, hate loses its power. Division crumbles. This is the healing message the world has feared: that Black people rising is not about flipping the roles of oppressor and oppressed. It's about dissolving the entire system. It's not about control—it's about balance. It's not about vengeance—it's about vision.

Unity is not about making everyone the same. It's about recognizing the beauty in our differences while remembering that all energy comes from the same divine source. A unified people, especially a spiritually awakened

Black people, represents a threat to a world built on lies, greed, and illusion. That's why the systems fight so hard to keep us asleep.

We are not just Black bodies trying to survive in a white-controlled world. We are divine souls remembering our true power. That power is amplified when we come into unity, not just with one another, but with the divine frequency that created us. Unity doesn't mean uniformity. It means alignment. It means flowing in the same direction—toward healing, toward truth, toward light. That starts inside each one of us.

The more we love our neighbor as ourselves, the more we dissolve the illusion of separation. The more we embrace our divine essence, the more we lift the veil for others to see. This is the true revolution—not a war of flesh, but a return to spirit. Christ consciousness is what it means to believe in Jesus.

Plate XII — Revelations of the Heavens

Chapter 12
Revelations of the Heavens

As we awaken into love and rise in Christ consciousness, the world around us begins to shift. Old systems tremble. Old beliefs collapse. The illusions that held humanity captive cannot survive in the presence of awakened minds. Awakening does more than heal the heart—it opens the eyes. As the inner eyes open, so do the heavens.

We are approaching a time when the truth that was hidden above us will be revealed below us. A time when humanity will be forced to confront what religion never prepared us to face—that we are not alone, that the universe is alive, and that the gods of this world were never the Creators of all worlds.

- This is the revelation that is coming.
- We must be spiritually ready for it.

The Days of Unveiling

There will come a day when the veil between heaven and earth shall be torn, and the rulers of this world shall confess openly: "We are not alone." This confession shall send tremors throughout the nations, for the foundations of false religion were built upon the belief that humanity is the center of all creation. But Elohim never said such things. For the Word declares, "The heavens declare the glory of God; and the firmament sheweth His handywork" (Psalm 19:1 KJV). The heavens declare—they speak, whisper, communicate, reveal. Every star is a witness. Every world is a testimony. Elohim's universe was never silent.

The Day When Humanity Looks Up

When disclosure arises, fear will seize many hearts. For it is written, "Men's hearts failing them for fear, and for looking after those things which are coming on the earth." (Luke 21:26 KJV).

This prophecy does not speak of storms or wars—but revelations. Things coming on the earth: arrivals, manifestations, visitors from realms long hidden. So when the heavens open, those anchored in flesh will tremble. However, those rooted in Spirit shall stand. For fear belongs to the physical mind. Strength belongs to Christ consciousness.

The Revealing of All Secrets

Luke 8:17 (KJV)—"For nothing is secret, that shall not be made manifest; neither any thing hid, that shall not be known and come abroad."

Matthew 10:26 (KJV)—"Fear them not therefore: for there is nothing covered, that shall not be revealed; and hid, that shall not be known."

Jesus (the spiritual Christ, not the physical man) foretold a time when every hidden system would be exposed. Alien disclosure is part of that unveiling—not a threat but a fulfillment. YHWH's systems of fear and physical worship cannot survive exposure.

Christ consciousness sees disclosure as awakening, not danger.

The revelation of extraterrestrial life shows humanity that the universe is spiritual, not controlled by a single physical tribal deity.

YHWH and the Gods of the Earth

Disclosure will unveil a truth long concealed: YHWH is not Elohim, and YHWH is not the Creator of the universe. For YHWH spoke from mountains, wrapped in fire, thunder, and smoke. He ruled through commandments, sacrifice, punishment, and fear.

- Elohim spoke before time.
- He spoke before matter.
- He spoke before flesh.
- Elohim breathed light into the darkness.
- Elohim birthed Spirit before bodies.
- Elohim shaped consciousness before form.

The Scriptures testify, "God is a Spirit: and they that worship Him must worship Him in spirit and in truth." (John 4:24 KJV).

YHWH demanded worship of flesh—circumcision, sacrifice, blood, ritual, and obedience by law.

- Elohim awakens.
- YHWH controls.

In the days of disclosure, this difference will be impossible to hide.

When Disclosure Shakes the Foundations

When humanity sees beings not born of clay, not shaped from dust, not bound to death, questions will rise like smoke:

"Who created them?"

"Do they serve YHWH?"

"Is there One above the God of Israel?"

The answer shall thunder across the consciousness of the awakened:

- Elohim reigns above all realms.
- YHWH governs only the physical domain.

Extraterrestrial Life and the Realm of Elohim

Elohim did not limit life to a single planet.

Elohim filled the universe with consciousness.

Christ spoke of this when saying, "In my Father's house are many mansions" (John 14:2 KJV).

These "mansions" are not earthly houses—they are dimensions, worlds, realms of existence created long before Adam walked the soil. Some beings remained in the higher realm of light. Some descended into form. Some walked among stars unknown to man. Others passed through Earth in ancient times. This universe is alive:

- It is populated.
- It is structured.
- It is layered.

Humanity is only one of Elohim's creations:

- not the first
- not the only
- not the final

Why Disclosure Will Destroy the Old Systems

The systems of domination were built upon a single, fragile belief:

Earth is the center of creation. Once that belief dies, the powers of this world lose their authority. How can religion claim supremacy if there are other civilizations older and wiser? How can nations claim dominance if there are beings whose technology defies physics? How can YHWH claim to be the Most High when disclosure reveals millions of realms beyond his jurisdiction? Thus, the old order shall crack, and Babylon shall fall.

For prophecy speaks, "Therefore shall her plagues come in one day... for strong is the Lord God who judgeth her." (Revelation 18:8 KJV).

The collapse of the old world will not come by war—but by revelation.

Christ Consciousness as the Shield of the Awakened

When the nations tremble, those in Christ consciousness shall stand fearless. For Christ consciousness removes the illusion of physicality and returns the soul to its spiritual origin. Christ consciousness reveals:

- I am not my body.
- I am Spirit.
- I cannot be devoured.
- I cannot be deceived.
- I originate from Elohim.

For the Scriptures warn, "Be sober, be vigilant; because your adversary the devil, as a roaring lion, walketh about, seeking whom he may devour." (1 Peter 5:8 KJV).

- He may devour flesh.
- He may devour fear.
- He may devour those who worship the physical.

But he cannot devour consciousness.
Christ consciousness is the armor of the soul.
The power that stands firm when the world trembles.
The inner light that no deception can overpower.

A Warning for What Is Coming

Not all beings who travel within the heavens are aligned with light. Some serve lower realms. Some follow the vibration of YHWH's dominion—control, hierarchy, obedience, and fear. So humanity must learn discernment.

The Scriptures warn: "Beloved, believe not every spirit, but try the spirits whether they are of God." (1 John 4:1 KJV).

In the days of disclosure:

- Physical eyes will see.
- But spiritual eyes must interpret.
- Christ consciousness must guide.
- Elohim's voice must lead.
- Those unrooted in Spirit will be led by fear.
- Those rooted in Spirit will walk in authority.

The Comfort of the Awakened

Disclosure is not the end—it is the beginning of remembrance. For the awakened will understand:

- Elohim's creation is vast.
- Humanity is not alone.
- Consciousness is eternal.
- YHWH is not supreme.
- Fear is unnecessary.
- Spirit can never be conquered.
- Christ consciousness is the true foundation of power.

When the heavens open, let your heart not be troubled. For the return of cosmic truth is the return of spiritual memory. Those who walk in Christ consciousness shall guide the nations into a new dawn.

The unveiling of extraterrestrial life is not a threat:

- It is a revelation.
- It is the tearing of old lies.

- It is the collapse of physical religion.
- It reveals the subordinate authority.
- It is the remembrance of Elohim's infinite creation.
- It is the awakening of nations.

The ones chosen to lead this awakening are those who return to Christ consciousness:

The divine mind is within.

The light cannot be hidden.

The Spirit cannot be deceived.

The heavens are preparing to speak, and the awakened are preparing to answer.

The revelations of alien disclosure do not stand alone as isolated events. They are part of a much older pattern—a pattern of veiled truths resurfacing after ages of suppression. As humanity awakens to the reality that we are not the only creation in the cosmos, a deeper question arises: Why were these truths hidden?

The next chapter uncovers the concealed wisdom—the forbidden teachings, silenced stories, spiritual technologies, and cosmic truths that reconnect humanity to Elohim, the Divine Source. It reveals how the physical god sought to keep humanity bound to matter, while the true Creator called every soul to rise above it.

Plate XIII — Hidden Knowledge

Chapter 13
Hidden Knowledge

Breaking the illusion means reclaiming our divine identity. It means remembering that we were not created to serve systems—we were created to build sacred legacies, to heal generations, and to embody the Creator through every action, word, and thought. We can start by knowing thyself.

Reclaiming Stolen Wisdom

"Man, know thyself, and you shall know the gods."— Inscription from the Temple of Luxor, House of Life, Kemet (ancient Egypt). It was long before the name Socrates was ever written in a scroll, long before Greek philosophy became the cornerstone of Western education, and the principle "Know Thyself" was already carved in stone in Kemet, the ancient Black civilization that the world now calls Egypt.

This was not just philosophy. It was spiritual law. Our ancestors knew that. In the sacred Temple of Luxor, also called the House of Life, priests, healers, and initiates were trained in the divine mysteries. These temples taught that to know oneself was to reconnect with the divine blueprint—the God force within you. This was a holistic knowledge of your mind, body, soul, and cosmic purpose. The people of Kemet believed that the Creator, whom they called Neter or Netjer, dwelt within each human being. You were not separated from the divine—you were a living vessel of it.

To "know thyself" meant more than self-reflection. It meant remembering that you are not just fresh—you are frequency. Not just body, you are energy and light, created in the divine pattern of the universe.

Here's what they don't teach in school: The Greeks, including Socrates, Plato, and Pythagoras, studied in Kemet. They were initiated into Kemetic wisdom. Many of them even wrote about their time learning in Africa.

Today, "Know Thyself" is taught as a Greek philosophical idea. Socrates gets the credit. Kemet is ignored or made to seem like a myth. The dark-skinned people who built those temples are erased or whitened in the textbooks. The wisdom that once belonged to a deeply spiritual Black civilization is now branded as Western thought. Here are some of the Sacred Sciences of Kemet:

Science: The Alchemy of Divine Order

In Kemet, science wasn't separated from spirit—it was spirit in motion. The ancient Kemites built temples aligned with celestial bodies. The Great Pyramid of Giza, constructed with mathematical precision, is so exact in its alignment to the cardinal points and star systems that modern scientists still debate how it was done without today's technology.

Why? Because the Kemites understood that everything in the universe is frequency, vibration, and energy—concepts that quantum physics is only now catching up with. They didn't just study science. They lived it as a sacred reflection of the divine cosmos.

Math: The Language of the Gods

Long before Greek numerals, Kemet had a complete and complex mathematical system. They used it not only for accounting and architecture but for understanding the patterns of nature. Sacred geometry—the shapes and ratios found in flowers, seashells, even galaxies—was woven into their temples and artwork as symbols of divine intelligence. The "Flower of Life," a pattern etched into temple walls, was not decoration. It was the creation of a visual map, showing the blueprint of existence. To the Kemites, math wasn't numbers—it was universal law.

Medicine: Healing the Body and Spirit

Kemet's priests were also physicians, trained in both spiritual and physical healing. Their medical papyri document over 700 remedies, surgical procedures, and diagnostic techniques that would be considered advanced even today. They treated the mind and body together because they understood that illness often began in the soul. They used herbs, energy work, and sound vibration—tools now being rediscovered in holistic medicine. They believed that every human being had a ka (life force) and a ba (soul)—and true healing meant restoring harmony to both.

Astrology: The Cosmic Blueprint

Kemet gave birth to the zodiac and astrological mapping long before it appeared in Greek or Roman culture. The priests of Kemet studied the heavens not for entertainment, but for guidance. They believed that the stars and planets reflected the divine order on Earth. Temples were built to align with solstices and star risings—particularly Sirius, whose rising marked the sacred Nile flood and the start of their calendar.

They understood "As above, so below."

The movement of the stars reflected the movement of the soul.

Sacred Geometry: The Patterns of Creation

The pyramids were built with geometric proportions tied to divine ratios such as the Golden Mean (Phi) and Pi. Every triangle, square, and circle held spiritual significance. They encoded universal truths into physical form, believing that by building in harmony with divine math, they could bring heaven to Earth. The architecture of Kemet was a living prayer. A map back to the Source.

Metaphysics: The Science of the Invisible

Metaphysics in Kemet was the study of spirit, soul, energy, and consciousness. They spoke of Neters (divine principles)—not gods in the Western sense, but aspects of the One Source. These principles were expressed through archetypes like Ma'at (truth and balance), Tehuti (wisdom and writing), and Ausar (resurrection and divine kingship).

These teachings weren't myths. They were keys to unlocking higher consciousness. Initiates went through years of training to master the self and understand the hidden laws of energy, intention, and reality.

Philosophy: The Foundation of All Thought

Plato studied in Kemet. Pythagoras studied in Kemet. The Greeks credited their learning to the Black priests of this ancient land, but the philosophy of Kemet wasn't abstract. It was deeply practical and transformational. "Know Thyself" meant to become divine through self-realization. Ethics, balance, justice, and harmony were lived through Ma'at, not just spoken of.

- Western philosophy took pieces.
- Kemet had the whole of understanding.

When you realize your ancestors founded the sciences, shaped spirituality, and understood the universe with divine clarity, you begin to see that you are not a victim of history. You are the author of it. They erased this to make you think you were born to be a slave. Yet you were born of gods, kings, healers, architects, and mystics.

- You don't need to reclaim greatness.
- You are greatness—waiting to remember itself.

There comes a time when you must look in the mirror and ask: Am I truly free? Or am I just surviving inside a cage that's been made to look like a dream?

That question becomes the doorway to the next truth— because once you recognize the cage, you can no longer pretend that the illusion is your home. Your spirit begins to ache for something more essential, older, and more sacred than anything this world has offered you. And that longing is the first sign that you are ready for the next step: not just uncovering who you were… but reconnecting with the One who formed you before the world lied to you.

Plate XIV — Reconnecting with the Creator

Chapter 14

Reconnecting with the Creator

For Black people, this question is revolutionary. Because from birth, we are handed an identity that isn't ours. We're told who we are, how to act, what success looks like, and who our God is. None of it is rooted in truth. It's all part of the illusory system designed to keep us spiritually asleep and physically dependent. It's time to wake up. Remember:

John 15:19 (KJV)—"If ye were of the world, the world would love his own: but because ye are not of the world, but I have chosen you out of the world, therefore the world Hateth you."

Detoxing from this system is not just about protest—it's about personal power. It's a sacred rebellion. And it starts with these seven radical steps to cleanse your mind, body, and spirit from the lies we've been sold.

Romans 12:2 (KJV)—"And be not conformed to this world: but be ye transformed by the renewing of your mind..."

1. Reprogram the Mind—Reject the Program

We live in the age of digital prophets and silent prisons. Where your opinions are curated by code, and truth has become a matter of branding. We were all born into a world already at war—not between nations, but between programs of the mind. Jew. Gentile. Black. White. Believer. Skeptic. Each of us was handed a script. Each of us told who we are, what we must believe, and what we must fear. But what if the real enemy was not flesh and blood? What if the most dangerous form of control was never the sword... but the story?

We were all lied to, in different ways, but lied to nonetheless. Black people were told they were slaves first, not divine first. White people were told they were superior, without being told why or by whom.

Jews were told they were chosen but never taught what that truly meant in spirit. Gentiles were told they were outsiders—unless they surrendered their minds to religion. All of it served one purpose: to divide and conquer the image of God. Every group received a script. Every mind received a program. Every heart received a wound disguised as a belief system. Now the spell is breaking, and with it comes the responsibility to ask: Who am I without the lies?

2. Detox the Culture—Reclaim Your Identity

You were never meant to imitate your oppressor—you were meant to be your divine self, but the system taught you otherwise. It handed you false identities and called them traditions. They gave you holidays like Christmas not to celebrate joy, but to convince you that blessings come from a white man in a costume, not the divine spark within you. You learned that Christopher Columbus "discovered" a land that was already full of life, spirit, and people. You were taught to feast on Thanksgiving while ignoring the genocide it celebrates. You were told Easter was about resurrection, but never about the original Black stories of rebirth that long predated Rome.

They taught you to celebrate Independence Day—without telling you that you were still in chains when the fireworks went off. Even wedding traditions—white dresses, European rituals—were designed to erase our native customs of sacred union. It's time to wake up. Reclaim your culture. Reclaim your image. Wear your natural hair with pride. It's your crown, your signal to the world that you remember who you are. Black women, stop trying to look like the world's version of "pretty." You are already power, beauty, and wisdom wrapped in one. Stop dimming your light to fit in a world that profits from your silence. Study your ancestors—not only for their pain, but for their brilliance. African spirituality, Kemetian science, ancestral memory—these are not fantasies. They are the foundation.

They told you Black was ugly, so they could sell you white beauty. They told you Africa was poor, so you'd never search for your stolen inheritance. They made you long for

Paris and Europe but erased the legacy of Timbuktu. Now, you see the lie.

Go to Africa. Learn what they hid from you. Witness the genius and the glory. This is how you detox the culture: by rejecting the illusion and stepping into your truth.

3. Detox the Spirit

You don't need a building to find God. You need stillness. You need silence. Matthew 6:5–6 (KJV)—"Jesus tells us when thou prayest, thou shalt not be as the hypocrites are: for they love to pray standing in the synagogues and in the corners of the streets, that they may be seen of men. Verily I say unto you, They have their reward. But thou, when thou prayest, enter into thy closet, and when thou hast shut thy door, pray to thy Father which is in secret; and thy Father which seeth in secret shall reward thee openly." This means going into a quiet place and meditating, not for show but in secret. Meditate daily to silence the chaos and hear the divine voice inside.

Fast—not just for weight loss, but for spiritual clarity. When you fast, you weaken the grip of the world and strengthen the voice of your spirit.

1 Peter 5:8 (KJV)—"Be sober, be vigilant; because your adversary the devil, as a roaring lion, walketh about, seeking whom he may devour." This tells us to be mentally alert, clear-minded, and self-controlled. It's a call to avoid spiritual laziness or distractions, whether from sin, pride, or worldly pleasures. Stay watchful and aware. Vigilance means keeping your spiritual eyes open, recognizing that dangers exist and are often subtle or deceptive.

"Adversary" is a legal term, like a prosecutor or accuser, seeking to condemn or entrap. The system and our law enforcement are not just a general force of evil, but a being actively working against you.

We have to understand that the imagery of a roaring lion symbolizes threat, intimidation, and power. Lions roar to assert dominance and instill fear. The devil, likewise, uses fear, chaos, and temptation to intimidate and mislead. Our society is constantly on the move, watching for weaknesses, looking for those who are spiritually vulnerable—those he can deceive, destroy, or pull away from their divine purpose.

4. Cleanse Your Temple

Your body is not just flesh and bone—it is the sacred temple of the Most High. Yet for generations, we've been conditioned to treat this divine vessel like a trash can. Fast food, processed snacks, sugary drinks, artificial flavors, and preservatives—these are not foods; they are weapons in disguise. They are carefully marketed poisons, engineered for addiction, sickness, and spiritual disconnection.

1 Corinthians 3:16 (KJV)—"Know ye not that ye are the temple of God, and that the Spirit of God dwelleth in you?"

This is not just a metaphor. It is a wake-up call. If the Spirit of God dwells within you, then what you feed your body directly affects your spiritual power. You cannot pour divine energy into a polluted vessel. Cleansing the body is the first step toward reclaiming your health, clarity, and connection to Source.

Rethinking the Modern Diet

Have you ever asked where the idea of eating three meals a day came from? It didn't come from nature—it came from industrial schedules and consumer culture. The truth is that your body doesn't need constant feeding. It needs time to heal, rest, and digest. It can take 24 hours or more to fully digest one full meal.

Eating three meals a day—and then snacking in between—is like asking your body to run a marathon without ever stopping to breathe. It overloads your digestive system, burdens your organs, and invites disease.

Eliminate Sugar

Refined sugar is one of the most addictive, inflammatory substances in the modern diet. It weakens your immune system, feeds cancer cells, spikes insulin, and disrupts your mood. Remove it, and your energy will rise, your skin will clear, and your mind will sharpen. Try eating one meal a day. You will be shocked at how much better you feel.

Ditch Processed and Packaged Foods

If it comes in a box or a can, chances are it's been stripped of nutrients and pumped full of chemicals. These additives keep your body acidic and inflamed, creating a breeding ground for chronic disease. Choose foods that grow from the earth, not ones engineered in factories.

Eat Living Foods

Fruits, vegetables, herbs, and seeds are high-frequency foods. They are full of life force, enzymes, minerals, and healing power. Think: kale, sea moss, berries, ginger, garlic, wild greens. These are not just food; they are medicine.

Hydrate with purpose. Water flushes out toxins, lubricates your cells, and supports every vital function. Aim for at least one gallon a day. Add a squeeze of lemon or a pinch of sea salt to enhance mineral absorption and detoxification.

5. Detox the Wallet—Redefine Success

They sold us a lie and called it success. They told us it looked like money, fame, and flashing luxury. Said if we wore the right brands, drove the right cars, and posted the right image, we'd finally be somebody. Let's be clear—that's not wealth. That's bondage disguised as glory. We've been programmed to consume, not create. Conditioned to chase clout instead of purpose. We spend hundreds on shoes that never touch the sidewalk, and thousands on clothes just to impress people who don't even know our story.

We're draining our wallets and our spirits just to fit into a fantasy crafted by systems that never had our healing in mind. That illusion? It's the white man's definition of success—a baited trap built to keep us broke, distracted, and spiritually starved. We don't need to *fake it till we make it*. That mindset has us playing a role in someone else's show, chasing validation through things that lose value the moment we swipe the card. The truth is, if we're always trying to look rich, we'll never become truly wealthy. We have to remember that the house with the white picket fence was never our dream but the one we have been told is the goal of success.

Real wealth is freedom. Freedom of time. Freedom of thought. Freedom of spirit. Freedom to say no to a job that drains you. Freedom to spend your days building something that matters.

Mark 8:36 (KJV)—"What shall it profit a man, if he shall gain the whole world, and lose his own soul?"

6. Detox the Media—Break the Spell

We live in the age of illusion. A time where we think we're more connected than ever, but in reality, we're more divided, distracted, and drained than we've ever been. The screen is the new sorcery. Every time you unlock your phone, you're stepping into a world designed to keep you addicted, anxious, and apart from your true self.

Social media is not a connection—it's consumption. What you're consuming shapes what you believe, how you feel, and even how you see others. We don't talk to each other anymore. We text. We scroll past real people for virtual strangers. What's worse? The media we consume is saturated with fear, division, and negativity. For Black communities, it's even deeper.

Turn on the news, and Black faces are criminalized. Turn on the music charts, and we're encouraged to glorify violence, self-hate, and materialism. Look at the trending pages—how many positive stories about Black unity, brilliance, or spirituality do you see? That's not a coincidence. That's control.

The Digital Matrix Is Real—and It's Spiritual

We are not just being programmed mentally—we're being drained spiritually. Algorithms study you. They know what triggers you, what makes you sad, what makes you angry—and they feed you more of it. Why? Because rage and fear keep you online. Peace doesn't profit them. So it's time for a media detox—a fast for your soul.

Weaponized Imagery

Look at how shows and movies often portray Black people as criminals, hypersexual beings, or broken families.

It shapes how the world sees us—and how we see ourselves. News bias: Studies have shown that Black suspects are shown in handcuffs or mugshots more often than white suspects, even when charged with the same crimes. It creates a false perception of danger. The entertainment agenda: Music and movies that glorify violence, drug use, and sexual exploitation are heavily pushed to Black youth, while stories of spiritual power, historical greatness, and cultural unity are buried.

So How Do We Break the Spell?

- Unplug regularly: Choose a day each week to turn off all media—no phone, no TV, no news. Let silence cleanse your soul.
- Go outside: Touch the earth. Sit with nature. God is not on your screen—He's in the wind, the trees, and the stillness.
- Talk to people: Reconnect face-to-face. Smile. Make eye contact. Let love replace fear.
- Protect your spirit: Limit what enters your eyes and ears. Negative content changes your frequency.
- Consume consciously: Replace junk content with books, documentaries, music, or podcasts that uplift, teach, and enlighten.

7. Detox Your Energy

Every trauma is a memory stored in your body. Every grudge is an open wound in your spirit. Every unspoken emotion is a storm waiting to be heard. If you've ever felt heavy for no reason, anxious in peaceful places, or disconnected from your joy, chances are your energy is congested. Just like the body needs a physical detox, your spirit needs a spiritual cleanse. We've been taught to clean our homes, our cars, even our closets—but never our inner energy. Yet that's where the real battle is.

Detox Your Energy?

Your energy is sacred. Emotional baggage turns into physical sickness. A clogged spirit cannot rise.

Psalm 51:10 (KJV)—"Create in me a clean heart, O God; and renew a right spirit within me."

You can't elevate while carrying spiritual weight. The most powerful act of resistance in this toxic world is healing yourself.

How to Begin

Sound Therapy

Use healing frequencies (such as 528 Hz), gospel music, or jazz to clear stagnant energy. Sound is one of the oldest forms of spiritual cleansing.

Movement as Medicine

Yoga, stretching, dancing, or walking barefoot on the earth. This helps trapped energy exit the body.

Sacred Release

Write letters to those who hurt you—not to send but to release. Speak forgiveness aloud. Let God deal with the rest.

Breathwork

Inhale peace. Exhale pain. Do this consciously for 3–5 minutes.

Practice Forgiveness

Luke 6:37 (KJV)—"Forgive, and you shall be forgiven." Forgiveness is not weakness. It's a release. It's healing. It's obedience to God.

Meditation

Spend 10 minutes in silence every day. No phones. No talking. Just presence and breath.

Salt Baths and Showers

Add sea salt or Epsom salt to a bath to draw out energetic toxins. Pray while you cleanse.

Affirmations with Scripture

Speak life over yourself: 3 John 1:2 (KJV)—"Beloved, I wish above all things that thou mayest prosper and be in health, even as thy soul prospereth."

Honor the Shadow, Not Just the Light

As the ancient Ma'at and the Yin and Yang taught, life is about balance. You are both light and dark, positive and negative, joy and grief, faith and fear. To detox is not to deny your darkness, but to acknowledge and cleanse it. Your trauma is not your identity, it's your initiation.

Action Plan

- Schedule a "soul cleanse day" monthly.
- No screens.
- No noise. Just you, God, and your healing practices.
- Journal what you're releasing and what you're calling in.
- Replace toxic relationships and media with uplifting community, scripture, music, and nature.

Plate XV — From Poverty to Power

Chapter 15
From Poverty to Power

THE ECONOMIC AND SOCIAL RECLAMATION OF THE BLACK MAN IS a biblical mandate. The story of the Black man across the globe has too often been framed through the lens of oppression, brokenness, and systemic degradation. Yet hidden within the sacred texts of Scripture lies a divine roadmap for total reclamation—not only spiritual but economic and social.

The Black man is not called to permanent marginalization but to divine rulership, stewardship, and renewal. This chapter unveils the biblical foundation for economic and social restoration, positioning the Black man as a king, a builder, and a prophet.

Recognizing Divine Inheritance

The foundation of reclamation, the first step toward reclamation, is to embrace the truth of divine inheritance.

Ownership is a heavenly principle, ordained from the beginning.

Psalm 24:1 (KJV)—"The earth is the LORD's, and the fullness thereof; the world, and they that dwell therein."

Scripture makes it plain that dominion, stewardship, and resource ownership are not worldly ambitions but spiritual mandates. The Black man must reject the false narrative of eternal dispossession and reclaim the understanding that he is an heir of divine promise.

Galatians 3:29 (KJV)—"And if ye be Christ's, then are ye Abraham's seed, and heirs according to the promise."

Without reclaiming identity first, economic and social power cannot be fully realized. Know thyself.

The Curse of Economic Slavery—Breaking the Chains

The economic poverty experienced by Black communities worldwide is not merely systemic; it has spiritual roots.

Deuteronomy 28:48 (KJV)—"Thou shalt serve thine enemies… in hunger, and in thirst, and in nakedness, and in want of all things."

The conditions described in Deuteronomy mirror the reality of modern Black life: laboring for the benefit of others, existing in a cycle of deprivation, and yearning for economic freedom. True reclamation requires breaking these ancient chains—not through political pleas, but through spiritual obedience and economic mastery rooted in divine laws.

Building Cities and Nations—The Biblical Blueprint

The call is not merely to survive but to build.

Isaiah 61:4 (KJV)—"And they shall build the old wastes, they shall raise up the former desolations, and they shall repair the waste cities, the desolations of many generations."

Economic and social reclamation demand a nation-building mentality. Like Nehemiah surveying Jerusalem's ruins and rallying the people to rebuild (Nehemiah 2:17-18), the Black man must survey his desolate communities and lead their transformation through businesses, schools, governance, and infrastructure. Restoration is a divine commission. Economic empowerment flows through wisdom and innovation, and true wealth is built on wisdom.

1 Kings 10:23 (KJV)—"And King Solomon exceeded all the kings of the earth for riches and for wisdom." Solomon's wealth was not by chance—it was cultivated through divine wisdom, innovation, and righteous stewardship. Similarly, Black communities must prioritize financial education, entrepreneurship, technological mastery, and land ownership as sacred responsibilities. Innovation, not imitation, will be the cornerstone of future Black prosperity.

Overcoming the Psychological Warfare of Poverty

Economic chains are forged in the mind before they appear in the hand.

Proverbs 23:7 (KJV)—"For as he thinketh in his heart, so is he." To reclaim economic and social power, the Black man must first defeat the internalized programming of inferiority and helplessness.

Romans 12:2 (KJV)—"Be ye transformed by the renewing of your mind." Victory will be determined not only by policies or protests but by the cultivation of a new, sovereign consciousness. Today's Black communities must create economic sanctuary areas where wealth circulates, businesses thrive, and internal resources sustain the people through external turmoil.

The Role of the Church—From Spiritual Hospital to Empowerment Center

The Black church must evolve. It cannot merely be a sanctuary for spiritual healing. It must become a center for economic and social power.

Isaiah 58:6 (KJV)—"Is not this the fast that I have chosen? To loose the bands of wickedness, to undo the heavy burdens, and to let the oppressed go free." The church must teach entrepreneurship, wealth building, land acquisition, and leadership as sacred responsibilities. Economic strength must become part of spiritual discipline, not a separate worldly endeavor.

The Prophetic Role of the Black Man

The Black man is called not just to survive history but to prophesy the future through action.

Obadiah 1:21 (KJV)—"And saviours shall come up on mount Zion to judge the mount of Esau; and the kingdom shall be the LORD'S." Prophets are not just preachers; they are builders of systems, challengers of injustice, and revealers of hidden truths. Reclaiming economic and social power is an act of prophetic resistance and divine fulfillment.

Wealth with Righteousness: Avoiding the Pitfalls of Wealth

Without purpose leads to destruction. The Black man's reclamation must avoid the traps of greed, pride, and materialism.

Mark 8:36 (KJV)—"For what shall it profit a man, if he shall gain the whole world, and lose his own soul?" Wealth must be viewed as a tool for communal empowerment, service, and the glorification of God, not mere personal indulgence. True success is measured not by accumulation but by righteous stewardship.

Plate XVI — The Future

Chapter 16
The Future

What Happens When We Wake Up?

We are standing at the edge of a new era. When we talk about Black people waking up, we are not simply speaking about increased pride or self-love. We are talking about the activation of a dormant spiritual technology, a frequency encoded into our very DNA that has been lying silent, waiting for the appointed time. Waking up means we no longer just know facts about our greatness—we embody it.

It means walking with the authority of knowing we are not fighting for scraps in a rigged system, but restoring a divine inheritance that was never truly lost—only forgotten. Once activated, this divine energy cannot be contained by political borders, religious divisions, or economic chains. It transcends nations. It transcends languages. It is the vibration of creation itself reclaiming its throne.

The Sacred Shift: Returning to Cosmic Order

This awakening is not just about righting racial wrongs—it is about restoring Ma'at: balance, harmony, truth, and cosmic justice. The future will not simply be Black people thriving within a corrupt system. The future will be the dismantling of corrupt systems altogether.

Imagine:

Education systems that teach universal truths and ancient wisdom, not colonial propaganda. Economic systems based on community empowerment and natural abundance, not exploitation. Governance is rooted in spiritual principle, not domination and deceit.

Healing practices that honor the body's sacredness, not poison it for profit.

This isn't a utopian fantasy. This is the realignment of Earth with divine law.

Isaiah 14:5–7 (KJV)—"The LORD hath broken the staff of the wicked, and the sceptre of the rulers. He who smote the people in wrath with a continual stroke, he that ruled the nations in anger, is persecuted, and none hindereth. The whole earth is at rest, and is quiet: they break forth into singing."

The Restoration of Spiritual Sovereignty

For too long, Black people have been spiritual refugees, practicing religions that strip away their power instead of restoring it. The future of the awakened will be marked by spiritual sovereignty: no more intermediaries between the soul and the Creator. No more doctrines designed to shame or disempower the people, but doctrines rooted in love.

The awakened will worship in spirit and truth, as in John 4:24 (KJV)—"God is a Spirit, and they that worship him in spirit and truth."

True worship will no longer happen inside buildings of stone, but inside bodies of light. The temples are returning—and they are walking among us.

Global Ripples—How Black Awakening Shifts the Whole World

When the original people awaken, the Earth itself responds. Environmental healing accelerates because the consciousness that reveres nature remembers. Global economies shift as materialism loses its grip and sustainable, soul-centered models rise. Reemerging political systems shake because the populations once considered "manageable" no longer consent to manipulation. Religious institutions fracture as seekers demand authentic connection over empty tradition. The Black awakening is not isolated—it catalyzes a global realignment. We will not simply change Black communities. We will change human destiny itself.

The Collapse of the False Self

As awakening spreads, people—Black and otherwise—will be forced to confront the false self they have built. The persona is crafted for survival in a sick society—the masks worn to fit into systems that despised them. The dreams were dreamed for acceptance rather than authenticity. Letting go of the false self will not come easily—it may feel like dying. Yet in that death lies true freedom.

In the new world, authenticity becomes the currency, integrity the measure of wealth, and spiritual clarity the highest status. Those who refuse to let go of illusion will slowly fade into the shadows of their own denial.

Conclusion

Before You Go

To the Black Man:

"Remember who you are. You are not what the world told you to be; you are what the Most High created you to be. Your journey through bondage was not because you were lesser, but because you were chosen, and like the old one, you forgot your divine covenant. You were given power, knowledge, and purpose, but when you exchanged them for conformity, the consequences followed. But this is not the end. This is your awakening. Rise now, not in bitterness, but in wisdom. Learn again, reclaim the truth that was hidden from you. You are not a victim of fate, but a child of the divine, called to lead with light, not revenge."

To the White Man:

"You were not born to hate. That seed was planted by a force that feeds on division, control, and fear. True power does not oppress; it uplifts. You, too, have a choice: to continue the legacy of domination, or to step into the higher law of love. Love does not erase history, but it redeems it. Let go of superiority. Choose truth over pride. Let healing begin by acknowledging harm and walking in humility."

To Both:

The war is not between flesh and blood, but between spirit and deception. It is not Black vs White—it is truth vs lies, love vs fear. When both rise, when the Black man remembers, and the White man repents, then the chains fall. Then and only then does freedom become real for all.

Micah 4:5 (KJV)—"For all people will walk every one in the name of his god, and we will walk in the name of the LORD our God forever and ever."

Love is the divine current flowing between all things— light and dark, masculine and feminine, seen and unseen. It is not weakness or emotion, but the very power that holds the universe together. Creation is love in motion, and balance is love expressed. When we awaken to this, we no longer fear the dark or worship only the light—we honor both as sacred because they are one.

Suggested Reading and Parallels

THE INTERPRETATIONS PRESENTED IN *THE VOICE OF Poverty—The Hidden War for Power* are original to the author.

However, readers interested in exploring historical, theological, and philosophical works that discuss themes parallel to those in this book may find the following sources insightful. These works and traditions have addressed related ideas through their own lenses, though the perspectives within this book remain independent.

Chapter 1: The First Creation

While this chapter offers a unique spiritual interpretation of humanity's origin, parallel ideas appear in Afrocentric scholarship (e.g., Cheikh Anta Diop's works on African origins), Gnostic cosmology (e.g., *The Apocryphon of John* from the Nag Hammadi Library), and comparative mythology studies.

Chapter 2: The Other Creation

Concepts resembling an "imitation creation" can be found in Gnostic texts such as *The Hypostasis of the Archons*, as well as symbolic interpretations within esoteric Christianity and certain Nation of Islam narratives.

Chapter 3: The Serpent

This reframing of the serpent as a liberator echoes in alternative interpretations of Genesis found in Kabbalistic mysticism, Gnostic thought, and feminist theological writings.

Chapter 4: The Tower of Babel

Similar symbolic readings of Babel as an allegory for unity and divine awakening can be found in Pan-Africanist thought, mystical Judaism, and certain postcolonial theological perspectives.

Chapter 5: Satan

The portrayal of a spiritual architect manipulating physical systems parallels motifs in apocalyptic literature, liberation theology, and writings on systemic oppression.

Chapter 6: Two Versions of Jesus— The Flesh vs. the Spirit

The distinction between a historical figure and a universal spiritual principle has been explored in Gnostic Christianity, metaphysical spirituality, and comparative religion studies.

Chapter 7: The Suppression

Historical accounts of cultural erasure and identity suppression appear in works on colonialism, the transatlantic slave trade, and indigenous resistance narratives.

Chapter 8: A Secret History

This theme closely parallels the Babylonian *Ludlul Bēl Nēmeqi* (The Babylonian Job).

Chapter 9: The Flip

The truth turned into a tool of control is present in postcolonial theory, semiotics, and critiques of imperial religion.

Chapter 10: The Power of Knowledge

The emphasis on knowledge as liberation parallels themes in Enlightenment philosophy, Pan-African activism, and spiritual self-mastery teachings.

Chapter 11: Waking Up with Love

This theme aligns with non-dual philosophies, Sufi mysticism, and inter-spiritual movements promoting unity consciousness.

Chapter 12: Revelations of the Heavens

This theme aligns with *Corpus Hermeticism* (Hermetic philosophy), which explores universal life and divine consciousness.

Chapter 13: Hidden Knowledge

The uncovering of suppressed truths resonates with historical revisionism, critical race theory, and esoteric research traditions.

Chapter 14: Reconnecting with the Creator

Parallels may be found in mystical Christianity, Hindu Vedanta, and Taoist teachings on spiritual return.

Chapter 15: From Poverty to Power

The concept of spiritual and material reclamation echoes Black economic empowerment movements, liberation theology, and the revival of ancient wisdom traditions.

Chapter 16: The Future

Visions of a transformed humanity align with utopian literature, prophetic traditions, and New Age eschatology.

About the Author

Samuel Messias is the author of *The Voice of Poverty: The Hidden War for Power*. His work explores spiritual awakening, Christ consciousness, and the movement from fear-based perception into love-based awareness. Through reflection and scripture, he encourages readers to seek truth within and rediscover the deeper spiritual meaning behind the teachings of Christ.

Continue the journey at

www.voiceofpoverty.com